Brain-Based Early Learning Activities

Published by Redleaf Press
10 Yorkton Court
St. Paul, MN 55117
www.redleafpress.org

First edition 2010
Cover design by Jon Letness
Cover photograph by Thinkstock.com
Interior typeset in Whitman and designed by Percolator
Printed in the United States of America
17 16 15 14 13 12 11 10   1 2 3 4 5 6 7 8

Library of Congress Cataloging-in-Publication Data
Darling-Kuria, Nikki.
    Brain-based early learning activities : connecting theory and practice / Nikki Darling-Kuria. — 1st ed.
        p. cm.
    Includes bibliographical references.
    ISBN 978-1-933653-86-0 (alk. paper)
    1. Cognitive learning. 2. Brain. 3. Effective teaching. 4. Early childhood education. I. Title.
LB1062.D36 2010
370.15'2—dc22   2009043110

Printed on acid-free paper

Brain-Based
Early Learning Activities

Connecting Theory and Practice

Nikki Darling-Kuria

Redleaf Press®
www.redleafpress.org
800-423-8309

To my dad for always believing in me even when I didn't believe in myself.
For encouraging me even when I didn't think something was possible.
For giving me the greatest gift a father could give his daughter: his time.
And for teaching a little redheaded rabbit how to use her brain!

Contents

ACKNOWLEDGMENTS

This book never would have been possible without the tremendous support of my family and friends. I'd like to thank Jeff A. Johnson, who believed enough in my talent to put his reputation on the line and recommend my work to Redleaf Press. I am eternally grateful to all of my mentors (I am so blessed there are many!), who have encouraged me along the way, and to the entire Redleaf Press team and David Heath and Kyra Ostendorf, my editors there, particularly for allowing me to work with developmental editor Jean Cook. Her guidance and deft skill have meant the world to me.

I'd especially like to thank some very special friends who have given me support above and beyond the call of friendship. Thank you, Jenn Vaughn, for being there for me, giving me the time to write this book and listening to me whine for hours on end about how I still wasn't finished! You have no idea how much your support meant to me. I'd also like to thank Amy Groves for being my personal stylist and Mary Kemp for making me feel like a supermodel (without the eating disorder).

A special thank-you goes out to all the little friends I've had bless my life through my family child care program. They have changed everything I had ever believed about what was possible. Brandon, Kevin, Holly, and Sarah will always hold a special place in my heart for being the children who helped me get going. And to Hayden, little Noah, Alec, Max, Ben, Eli, Taylor, Jordyn, Tanner, Maddison, and Simmone for keeping me going.

Being a student at Pacific Oaks College has changed my life (thank you, Sue Williamson!). I have met many extraordinary people who have encouraged me and helped me fine-tune my voice. I'd specifically like to thank Gustavo Gonzales for providing the clarity I needed at a crucial time when I couldn't see straight.

I've been fourteen years without my mother, and I am still missing her. Mom, I hope I made you proud.

To my children I cannot say thank you enough for your help (Will typed the bibliography, Elyse fact-checked the glossary, and Caitlin helped select some activities and designed some of the brain graphics). You have been and continue to be my inspiration for everything I do and for all that I will ever become. The three of you are the best teachers this student has ever had.

Saving the best for last, I have to honor the love of my life for giving me time, space, patience, understanding, blind faith, and enduring love. I never, ever could have undertaken this project without the support of my husband, Josh Kuria. He is the kindest soul and deepest believer in all things that are possible. He doesn't see his family as we are today; through his eyes he sees us as already being whom we can become. He holds our hands and our hearts when we need his strength to go out and change the world.

INTRODUCTION

You probably know some people who seem outgoing and spontaneous, some who are thoughtful and analytical, and others who seem wired to be creative. The truth is that, although we don't have any control over our eye color or our gender, we can change our wiring. We are wired to be works in progress.

A newborn baby has only a partially developed brain yet about the same number of neural connections as adults have. That number nearly triples by age three, although it is at that point that we begin to shed unused neural connections. Can you imagine? At age three we already begin to experience "use it or lose it."

The good news is that we do this in phases, and during certain phases we start over—in a sense. Periods of pruning in one region of the brain often prompt development in a different region. For example, when children hit puberty, different regions of the brain begin developing (Medina 2008).

Brain-Based Learning Research

Eric Jensen, as both teacher and scientist, has not only researched the field of neuroscience but also tested brain-compatible learning theories in a classroom with school-age children. He has authored more than twenty books about the applications of brain research to education (see References, pages 194–95). In his book *Teaching with the Brain in Mind* (1998), Jensen describes the model of brain-based learning and the importance of understanding how the brain learns in order to apply appropriate teaching strategies when working with young children. According to Jensen (2007), brain-based teaching is the application of strategies that appear to be compatible with the brain based on research findings.

Brain-compatible learning requires taking a holistic approach to helping a child learn to develop his whole brain (Jensen 2007). This means that everything, including the environment and the games and activities that are presented to children, is intentional and designed to compel children to use their whole brains. Unlike traditional learning theories that focus on linear development, brain-based learning engages the whole brain in cognitive and physical development simultaneously. A linear activity that involves only movement or language would use only one hemisphere of the brain. In contrast, an activity that combines movement and language requires both hemispheres of the brain to become engaged.

An example of this would be using your elbow to write your name in the air. As your elbow forms the letters of your name and moves through the air to spell it, the brain is making a connection between the physical movement and the cognitive movement. If you use your right elbow to write your name from left to right, you will cross the midline of your body, which sends a message to your left brain that you want it to get involved. These kinds of intentional actions help make concrete neurological connections (Jensen 2007).

The Importance of Emotional Memory

To further explain brain-based learning, I will describe how the brain stores emotional memory. Take any event of national significance, and ask someone what she was doing during the time she learned of the event. Specifically, President Kennedy's assassination, the shooting of President Reagan, the crash of the space shuttle *Challenger*, the events of September 11, 2001, and more recently the election of President Barack Obama are most often remembered (or will be remembered) with graphic detail. People often remember such events in detail and what they were doing when they learned of them—right down to the sensory level of what they could taste, smell, hear, touch, and see. Conversely, if you were to ask someone what she was doing on a specific date with no emotion attached to it, chances are she will have no idea what she was wearing, what the weather was like, or any other sensory recollection of that day. The brain stores emotional memory first because of the impact emotions make on the memory. Emotions create multisensory responses that attach to the memory and create a broader opportunity for recall. Most people know these facts about emotional memory intuitively, even if they haven't thought of them in these terms.

When you work with young children, keep in mind the importance of emotional memory. Any threat to the child can create a negative emotional memory. A good experience, though, can leave a positive emotional memory (Sousa 2006). The best way I can illustrate this is with a story.

It was a cool fall day, and I was chaperoning my daughter's Brownie troop on a much anticipated field trip. We were visiting an alpaca farm. Elyse loves animals so much that she wants to be a veterinarian when she grows up, and she wants to help care for police and military service animals. Being good with animals is important to Elyse. After showing us around the farm, the farmer asked if anyone in the group was brave enough to lead an alpaca through an obstacle course. Elyse was excited to get the chance to handle a live animal. She was chosen right away. Things were going fine until Elyse got the rope to lead the alpaca all by herself onto the course. Suddenly the alpaca jumped up. Elyse got scared, so she dropped the rope but then immediately realized her mistake. The alpaca ran away, and Elyse started to cry. She ran to the back of the barn and refused to come back to the group.

I went to her, looked her in the eyes, and said, "Elyse, what happened is okay. The farmer caught the alpaca, no one was hurt, and everything is fine. Do you want to come back and try again?"

She shook her head and said emphatically, *"No!"*

So I continued, "Elyse, if you choose not to go back and try again, this is where the memory of this day ends for you. All you will remember is that the alpaca got away. Every time you think of this memory, you will feel sad again, but it's not too late to change the memory. If you go back right now, grab ahold of that lead rope, and hold on tight, you can still take the alpaca on a walk through this obstacle course, and that will be the memory that will stay with you. Which one is it going to be?"

She wiped her eyes and looked back at the farmer waiting with the rope in hand. She plucked up her courage and headed straight back to the alpaca, determined not to let go this time. She held on tight and led the alpaca through a maze, up a teeter-totter, and around a figure eight.

Today whenever someone mentions an alpaca, instead of saying, "An alpaca got away from me once," Elyse says, "I got to lead an alpaca once." She learned a lot that day—alpacas are strong, you have to hold on tight, and they can jump and run fast. But she also learned that she could change the kind of memory she could have had about that day. In the end, she made the right choice.

Storytelling is a perfect example of how children (and adults) can construct brain-based learning. Everyone has a story to tell, and good storytelling comes from life experience. Using open-ended dialogue to tell a story helps children build a world based on what they know. When you listen to their stories, you also begin to get an understanding of what it is they know. But I'm not talking about assessment here; I'm talking about building strong brains.

The example of how Elyse learned something about herself from her experience with the alpaca created a framework for how I thought about Lev Vygotsky's theory that children construct learning from their prior experiences. Vygotsky, a Russian psychologist (1896–1934), developed the idea that children are able to acquire progressively more complex mental abilities if they have the correct tools of the mind (Bodrova and Leong 2007).

A tool can be used to solve a problem. Helping children develop tools of the mind is a way to help children become lifelong problem solvers. I remember hearing a phrase attributed to psychologist Abraham Maslow: "It is tempting, if the only tool you have is a hammer, to treat everything as if it were a nail" (1966, 15). To me this meant that if I didn't have the appropriate tools in my mental tool kit, I wouldn't be effective at solving all of my problems. It was my prior learning about my problem-solving skills that helped me put this phrase into context. I knew that sometimes I could solve problems on my own, but I also knew that sometimes I needed help. My tools could be my own mental strategies, or they could simply be knowing which sources to go to for help.

The Positive Effects of Brain-Based Learning

As children progress through their early years and head into school, brain-based learning can continue to have a positive influence on them. According to Connell, in *Brain-Based Strategies to Reach Every Learner* (2005), teaching and learning are all about making connections. She explains how understanding theories such as Howard Gardner's multiple intelligences can have a profound impact on how teachers approach students with different intelligences.

Gardner's hallmark work on multiple intelligences (MI) counters the notion that there exists but a single human intelligence that can be assessed by standard psychometric instruments. Gardner contends that humans exist in a multitude of contexts and that these contexts require different approaches to foster their development.

Through his work studying gifted and typical children, adults without disabilities, and adults with brain injuries he began to develop two separate streams of research that led him to his multiple intelligences theory. Gardner believed there could be a more naturalistic approach to understanding how people gain skills and knowledge. He felt that tests were not the best way to ascertain specific information about a person's intellect.

Gardner's multiple intelligences theory has eight areas of focus:

1. Linguistic: focuses on words and language

2. Musical: focuses on music, sound, and rhythm

3. Logical-Mathematical: focuses on logic and numbers

4. Spatial-Visual: focuses on space and images

5. Bodily-Kinesthetic: focuses on body movement

6. Interpersonal: focuses on other people's feelings

7. Intrapersonal: focuses on self-awareness

8. Naturalist: focuses on natural environment (Gardner 2004)

Each area has its own unique place in the brain. Understanding this can help teachers target learning that reaches students at the most opportune times in their development. According to Gardner, each of the multiple intelligences has a physiological location in the brain. When children engage in activities that involve creating music (making sounds), they are activating the auditory cortex located in the temporal lobe. However, the processing of sound (specifically the pitch) triggers connections in the frontal and parietal lobes and in both hemispheres. The act of making sounds is akin to sending out a search plane to find areas of the brain to connect with, and which connections the brain is able to make depends on the stage of development the child is in. I'm getting ahead of myself with describing the different parts of the brain, but the point I'm trying to make here is that when we know how the brain is connected, we can develop child-specific curriculum.

Much of MI research has focused on how to use brain-based learning strategies in the classroom for children ages five and older. In the beginning I was unclear about how to provide activities that were expressly designed to deliver the right kind of stimulation to the right part of the brain to help make what is learned permanent for very young children.

Brain-Based Learning with Young Children

I discovered that learning patterns are set by age five and that the greatest opportunity for learning happens in the first three years of life. At that point I wondered why all these brain-based strategies I had read about focused on school-age children. If all that neural activity was happening from birth to three, couldn't we—or rather, shouldn't we—intentionally create environments designed with the brain in mind?

Whether we are talking about building an organization or a learning environment, relationships are the cornerstone. Children need to know that the person who leads them through their day is genuinely concerned with their emotional well-being. These strong emotional connections build self-esteem and help children construct social meaning as well. Although this book focuses on games and activities to help children learn about the world around them, we must not forget to value the child as an individual first. Ultimately, what is most important is what children come to learn about themselves.

I believe that adults can learn as much from children as they learn from us. Why then am I writing a book about brain-based learning when the children already know so much? I asked myself that question, and the answer I came up with was "because we adults haven't learned how important it is to teach with the brain in mind."

The one thing that really helps me put the pieces of new knowledge together is the ability to connect theory with practice. Perhaps because I teach both adults and children, I feel compelled to be able to explain why this particular brain-based strategy really helps people learn.

I distinctly remember going to a workshop in which the instructor said something like, "It's important to rock infants." The crowd collectively nodded affirmatively as though this information was nothing new. I looked around and wondered what I was missing. Everyone really seemed to take something away from this statement, but I wasn't so sure we understood why. So I asked, "Why?" It turns out the instructor admitted she didn't know. She said she just knew that people say it's important to hold and rock infants. Again, the crowd accepted this as fact, and she wanted to move on. Can you tell where this story is going?

I wasn't ready to move on; I wanted to learn more. I stuck my hand in the air again and asked the instructor if I could share what I knew as to why this piece of information might be helpful to the participants. Reluctantly she agreed, and I proceeded to explain why it is important to rock. The first and most obvious reason is the close bond formed when holding infants in our arms and gently rocking them. The second, less obvious is the stimulation rocking provides to the vestibular region of the inner ear. Research has proved that early stimulation to this region helps children gain weight faster and develop vision and hearing earlier (Jensen 1998). All this leads to earlier and more acute opportunities to develop written and oral language skills.

After I had spoken, I looked around at the attendees and saw "deer in the headlights" eyes staring back at me. I often let my enthusiasm for learning overtake my ability to be tactful. In that moment I believed that the participants needed to hear the theory behind the practice so that they could direct their interactions with infants in the most effective way. I wasn't sure my response was what the participants wanted to hear (and certainly not what the instructor wanted to hear), and without further explanation this tidbit probably fell short of making it into anybody's long-term memory. But I couldn't leave that notion hanging that there isn't a concrete reason why infants are rocked. I thanked the instructor for allowing me to share and slowly sank back down into my seat, all the while wishing my enthusiasm for learning about brain development was contagious.

My Approach to Brain-Based Learning

Shortly after that experience, I decided to write this book for early childhood professionals to help them learn how the brain functions and to provide brain-compatible curriculum for young children. Because infants come into this world as holistic learners, we should do everything in our power to help ensure that they get a holistic education. It is imperative that we understand how they develop as humans, starting with the brain, the organ that makes them the complex creatures they are.

PART 1: THEORY

This book is divided into two parts. The first part provides the foundation for understanding the theory of brain-based learning as it relates to creating early learning activities for young children.

Chapter 1 provides an overview of the parts of the brain and how they affect learning and memory. This chapter provides the framework for understanding what the different parts of the brain need for learning to take place.

Chapter 2 explains the key components necessary to create a brain-based early learning environment. This environment creates the stage on which all your brain-based teaching and a child's learning performances will take place.

PART 2: PRACTICE

The book's second part addresses the practice of brain-based learning. It includes activities in eight learning domains.

In chapter 3 I discuss how a child learns in a brain-based early learning environment and what strategies are effective in developing executive function in the brain.

Chapter 4 comprises the brain-based activities divided into eight learning domains:

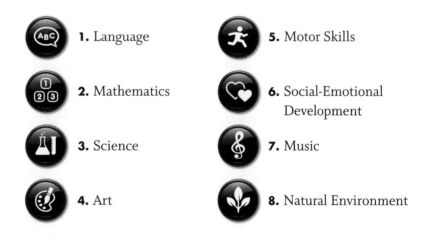

1. Language
2. Mathematics
3. Science
4. Art
5. Motor Skills
6. Social-Emotional Development
7. Music
8. Natural Environment

"Learning domains," also thought of as categories of study, describe different areas of educational activities. Each learning domain is introduced by brain-compatible learning strategies to help you prime your young learners. Using these strategies will help children learn new ways to use their brains when doing the activities described in each domain.

The individual activities have been chosen specifically for the way they create brain-compatible experiences for young children. To be truly brain-compatible activities, most activities should fall into more than one of these domains.

I've placed each activity into the category that represents its primary learning domain. To help link the activities and suggest how you could use an activity to address a different domain, all applicable symbols are listed at the top of each activity. Each activity also includes:

- the age range of targeted learners
- a list of required materials
- suggestions for diversity adaptation and multisensory experiences
- extension ideas for further exploration

At the end of the book, I've included a glossary and a list of references. The glossary defines key terms used throughout the text. The references give full publication information for all sources I cite in the book, providing you with further reading opportunities to expand your understanding of brain-based learning.

————

I hope you enjoy this book and come to think of it as your partner in creating brain-compatible experiences for young children.

Theory

The Brain:
Its Parts and Their Functions in Learning and Memory

A parent once asked me, "What makes brain-based learning different from any other kind of learning?" I struggled at first to articulate exactly what makes brain-based learning different, but then it hit me. "It's all about building executive function." When I excitedly tried out this new explanation on my husband, he said, "Yeah, so? What does that mean?" What had seemed like an "aha moment" to me apparently still wasn't clear. I needed to add details about what "executive function" is to help make my point.

Executive function is the processes of different parts of the brain to manage abstract and higher-order thinking as well as regulate the emotional system. That definition felt like a good start, but I still felt I needed more, so I added, "Brain-based learning is connecting new learning to what is already meaningful to a child." What this means is that when prior learning is intentionally directed at new skills in a brain-compatible learning environment, children are able to develop critical thinking skills and self-regulation of emotions. Both are vital skills necessary to achieve academic success and personal satisfaction through the development of healthy relationships.

To begin to create a framework for understanding how the brain learns, it is important to know about the parts of the brain and understand their functions in learning and memory. Let's start with the basics.

What the Brain Needs

The brain needs food, sleep, oxygen, water, and novelty and challenge to function. At a minimum, the brain needs water. In fact, the brain is mostly water, so it's important to continually hydrate our brains by drinking lots of water.

The brain needs nutrition. Eating *healthy* food, as opposed to *any* kind of food (read *junk food* here), is vital to healthy brain development. The glucose we get from fruit and from exercising gives us an especially good jolt of energy to accomplish more learning. The brain needs healthy food.

The brain needs sleep. During sleep our brain not only recharges but also tackles the big job of organizing the day's activities into "files" within the brain. It takes anywhere from four to twelve hours to process new skills and place them in a permanent storage file. If you don't give your brain enough rest, it isn't able to complete this important job. The files pile up (as they do in my office), and as a result you might have trouble remembering how to do things or where you put important stuff. The brain needs rest.

The brain needs oxygen. Oxygen is food for the brain, and it consumes more during intense periods of mental activity. Just like during physical exercise when the body needs oxygen to power the muscles, the brain needs oxygen to boost memory, concentration, and even balance. Clean oxygen, free from contaminants such as smoke, dust, and allergens, provides food power for the brain. The brain needs oxygen.

The brain needs novelty and challenge. The brain relies on novelty to keep it engaged and awake. And when challenged in a way that is absent of fear or threat, the brain works harder to form connections. The brain needs stimulation.

How the Brain Works

The brain processes different types of new information through different pathways. Generally pictures, text, and spoken words reach our brains through our senses. Thinking of the brain as a computer is one of the easiest comparisons to use when discussing how information is transferred or "routed." Start by thinking of the way information is initially processed through a "server," which is the brain's thalamus. Then the data is sent simultaneously to different "hard drives"—different brain regions—depending on what type of information is being processed. Language is sent to the temporal lobe, visual images are sent to the occipital lobe, and if any threatening messages are coming in, the amygdala is triggered. The amygdala will stimulate the nervous system to get the quickest response (Jensen 2008).

The frontal lobe holds our short-term memory, while the brain decides what to do next. New data is held there for five to twenty seconds, and then, if it is deemed irrelevant, it is dismissed and not retained. If the new information is worth remembering, the brain sends it to the explicit memory, which is stored in the hippocampus, located in the middle brain. If this new explicit learning is considered worthy of long-term memory, it is sent to the cortex, which is located in the frontal lobe, the place where the whole process started. Think of all this "computer processing" as happening at lightning speed. But although the process of sending the new information to the appropriate place happens instantaneously, the process of filing and storing this new information can take days and even weeks to complete. This fact alone is why scaffolding is so critical in teaching and learning. Closely linked to Lev Vygotsky's theory of Zone of Proximal Development, scaffolding occurs when new learning is integrated into existing knowledge with the support of an adult. To ensure that what is learned becomes permanent requires repeated and reinforced exposure of the new information in novel ways.

To be intentional in how we create learning activities for children, we have to understand the parts of the brain, their functions, and how the brain learns and stores memory. If we want children to recall newly learned information at the exact time in which they need it, we have to be mindful of how we put it into their brains in the first place.

Parts of the Brain

Before we can begin to design a brain-based learning environment complete with brain-compatible activities, we need to spend some time learning about the brain itself. We need to look at it section by section to make sure we can see the road map that children follow as they develop. Don't worry—this is not a neuroscience course, so I'll be brief and highlight only the key areas.

Since the brain looks like a walnut, I like to point out the basic facts "in a nutshell." The average brain weighs only about three pounds and is the size of a grapefruit. It is wrinkled and has two hemispheres, four lobes, and more than a million miles of nerve fiber. It's squishy and fragile, and the one you have is the only one you'll ever have. As I pointed out before, because the brain is mostly water, drinking plenty of water is very important for brain development and function.

The brain stores different information in different places. As I mentioned, most new things learned are stored initially in short-term memory. Then if the information is deemed important, it will go on to long-term memory, where it can be recalled later. Information that is not recognized as being important will disappear. Repeated exposure to information helps compel the brain to transfer new information to long-term memory before it's lost.

As far as brain evolution and function are concerned, we actually have three brains:

1. lizard brain, or brain stem

2. mammalian brain, or middle brain

3. human brain, or cerebral cortex

The brain stem, also called the lizard brain, is the most ancient of the three brains. It regulates basic functions like breathing, waking and sleeping, and heart rate (Medina 2008). It includes your cerebellum, which regulates movement.

ANATOMY AND FUNCTIONS OF THE BRAIN

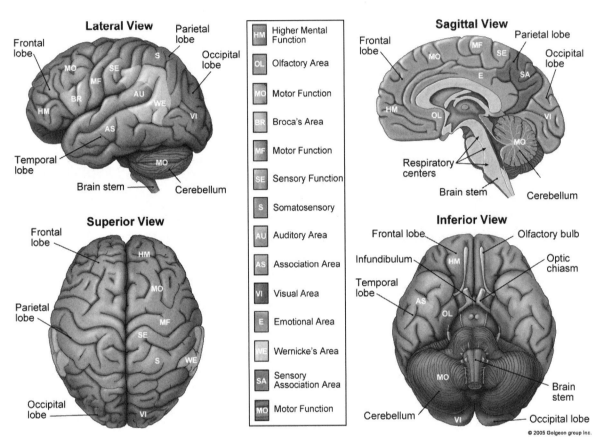

© 2005 Golgeon group Inc.

The middle brain, also called the mammalian brain, developed next. It is responsible for your "animal instincts." This means your basic survival depends on this brain region—your fight-or-flight instinct, your feeding instinct (think of how a baby is born knowing how to suckle), and your instinct to reproduce. It includes the limbic system, thalamus, hypothalamus, and amygdala, among other things.

Finally, on top of all of the other parts sits the cerebral cortex. This is your human brain. It is also the part that is called gray matter and looks all wrinkly and folded like a walnut. If you were to unfold it, the cortex would be the length of a baby blanket (Medina 2008).

Let's first look in more detail at the cerebral cortex with its complex interacting lobes and hemispheres. Later we'll revisit the middle brain, where a lot of emotional and memory processing occurs.

Human Brain, or Cerebral Cortex

The human brain, or cerebral cortex, is the largest part of the brain and controls memory, sensory interpretation, and higher-order thinking. This brain is responsible for conscious thinking, perception, thought and emotion, and awareness.

LOBES

Within the human brain or cerebral cortex, more commonly referred to as the cortex, are four areas called "lobes" that separate the different functions. The four lobes are the frontal, parietal, temporal, and occipital lobes. These lobes don't act independently. The four lobes connect to the brain stem's cerebellum, which regulates movement. The region where the lobes and cerebellum meet controls posture, balance, motor memory, and cognitive areas, such as counting and ordering. The lobes also interact with the middle brain's basal ganglia, which are a cluster of neurons that work to smooth muscle movement and anticipate what action to take next. Nevertheless, each of the four lobes has a separate function.

Frontal Lobe
The frontal lobe forms the front portion of the cerebral hemisphere. The motor areas control movements of the voluntary skeletal muscles. Association areas carry on higher intellectual processes, such as concentration, planning, problem solving, and judgment of the consequences of behavior. The area immediately behind the forehead is known as the prefrontal cortex, which is where executive functioning occurs.

Parietal Lobe
The parietal lobe is located just behind the frontal lobe in the cerebral hemisphere and is separated from it by a shallow groove, which serves a major landmark in the brain called the "central sulcus." This groove separates the primary motor and somatosensory cortex (Jensen 1998). Its sensory regions are responsible for the sensations of temperature, touch, pressure, and pain sensed by the skin. Its association areas work to create an understanding of speech and use of words to express thoughts and feelings

Temporal Lobe
The temporal lobe lies below the parietal lobe and behind the frontal lobe of the cerebral hemisphere and is separated from it by a shallow groove known as the "lateral sulcus" (Jensen 1998). Its sensory areas are responsible for hearing. Its association areas are used in the interpretation of sensory experiences and in the memory of visual scenes, music, and other complex sensory patterns.

Occipital Lobe

The occipital lobe forms the back portion of each cerebral hemisphere and is separated from the cerebellum by a shelflike extension, called the "tentorium cerebelli." There is no distinct boundary between the occipital lobe and the parietal lobe in front of it, or between the occipital lobe and the temporal lobe, which lies under it. The occipital's sensory areas are responsible for vision. The associated regions function to combine visual images with other sensory experiences. The visual cortex is located in this lobe and serves as a pathway for visual input.

CEREBRAL HEMISPHERES

The brain is divided into two hemispheres, the left and the right, which have distinct functions. Imagine dividing the brain down the middle, with equal parts of all four lobes on each side, or hemisphere. Each hemisphere then uses its half of each lobe to process that lobe's functioning in more specifically targeted ways.

<table>
<tr><td>

LEFT HEMISPHERE

Processes:
Sequentially
In Parts
Language
Logically
Differences

</td><td>

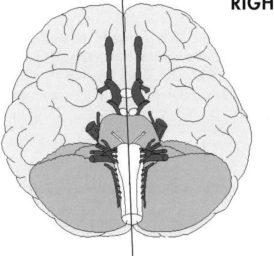

</td><td>

RIGHT HEMISPHERE

Processes:
Randomly
In Wholes
Spatial
Behavior
Intuitively
Similarities

</td></tr>
</table>

The left hemisphere learns in order, is better at processing language, works better with parts, and helps us make sense of our daily lives while inviting challenge. A region called the Broca's area is located in the frontal lobe of the left hemisphere. This region is responsible for the production of speech. The Wernicke's area is responsible for language comprehension and the production of meaningful speech. This region is also connected to the auditory cortex, which processes the spoken word.

The right hemisphere learns randomly and is better than the left hemisphere at processing pictures, colors, space, and perceptual information. It works better with wholes (meaning multiple ideas related to a concept versus just one part at a time) and processes negative emotion faster (Jensen 1998). Unlike the left brain, there are no specific "areas."

You're likely familiar with the long-discussed notion of "left-brain people" being methodical and practical and "right-brain people" being creative and free-spirited. In general this may be true, but no one uses one hemisphere exclusively. For example, a person who is interested in music might start listening to music or playing music as a right-brain activity, but if that person begins to study music and becomes, say, a classical pianist, this then becomes left-brain activity. Once an activity moves from the novel to the practical (and vice versa), it shifts its place within the hemispheres. This is a good thing! We want both sides of our brains communicating so that we can keep both sides as strong as possible.

It's important to remember that while each side has distinct functions, they freely exchange information back and forth. For example, the right hemisphere is where we experience negative emotions. Knowing that emotions can have a chronic negative effect on learning, and that the right brain is responsible for processing negative emotions, it's critical to develop learning activities that target the left brain to avoid the harmful impact of negative emotions.

Of course it's not that simple, because even left-brain activities can leave some children feeling negative emotions like those associated with anxiety and frustration. It's not a given that if you plan a novel, challenging activity that focuses on language processing, it will have a positive impact on each learner. It takes multiple opportunities for contact with each learner's hemispheres and lobes to create learning that will be a chronic positive force in her life.

Corpus Callosum

The corpus callosum is a broad, thick band consisting of millions and millions of nerve fibers connecting the right and left hemispheres. The fibers are axons of cells in the cerebral cortex. If something prevents those cells from developing, then the corpus callosum won't develop. Without this bridge of cells, the two hemispheres can't coordinate activities.

Mammalian, or Middle Brain

The middle part of the brain is where emotional processing takes place and where our memories are stored.

Emotional processing is not the only function of the middle brain. In fact, this part is primarily responsible for the functional region of the brain. In the middle brain the basal ganglia regulate motor functions by keeping muscles moving smoothly and continuously. They interact with the cerebral cortex's lobes and also transmit signals among the brain, spinal cord, and body.

LIMBIC SYSTEM

The limbic system is a complex set of structures that includes the thalamus, the hypothalamus, the amygdala, and the hippocampus. The limbic system appears to be primarily responsible for our emotional life and has a lot to do with the formation of memories as a result of the interaction between reason and emotion.

Thalamus

The thalamus is responsible for routing sensory input to the various parts of the brain. The thalamus processes all of the senses—except smell—before it sends the signal to any other part of the brain. It has often been likened to a computer server because it takes in all of the sensory input and reroutes it to the various parts of the brain. When we focus our attention on something, information begins to be exchanged from our eyes to our thalamus to our visual cortex, located in the occipital lobe. This back-and-forth is what directs our focus on something in particular.

Hypothalamus

The hypothalamus serves as the regulator for all body functions, including body temperature, hunger, thirst, and sleep. Deeply connected to the central nervous system, this region also coordinates hormonal and behavioral rhythms.

Amygdala

In the amygdala, the brain processes intense emotional response. It is within the amygdala where suspicion, fear, anxiety, and our fight-or-flight response dwell. This area of the brain serves as our first alert system. Nevertheless, because of emotions embedded in the brain, this system isn't always accurate. This area also performs memory consolidation.

Hippocampus

The hippocampus is responsible for cementing long-term memories. You probably have a basement or attic that has a lot of stuff in it that needs to be sorted and cleaned out, but you never have enough time to do it. The hippocampus does it every day! It has to keep the holding room clear for new learning that has made it past the working memory (the part of short-term memory that integrates, retrieves, processes and disposes of information) but may or may not make its way to long-term memory.

The hippocampus is finely attuned to whether these memories warrant a resting spot in the long-term memory. If the learning has meaning attached to it, the hippocampus has an easier time identifying whether it should move this new piece of information to long-term memory. If the hippocampus determines that a piece of information is not important (perhaps because it came into the holding room riding on too few neurons), the information will be deleted from our working memory and will not get to our long-term memory.

Our job as early educators is to help the hippocampus as much as possible by giving each child many opportunities to learn (through senses, building on prior learning, making meaning) so the new information moves quickly into long-term memory.

Brain Cells

In addition to all those parts of the brain I've just presented, we can't forget the bits that hold everything together. There are many kinds of brain cells made up of chemicals, tissue, proteins, and fats, but the two most common kinds of cells are glial and neurons.

GLIAL CELLS

Glial cells are responsible primarily for the transportation of nutrients and regulation of the immune system. These cells also produce myelin for the axons (see the section on the myelination process, next page). Glial cells are ten times as concentrated as neurons but are equal in their importance and function (Jensen 2008).

NEURONS

Neurons are the basic processing and structural components of the nervous system. Neurons cannot be seen with the naked eye: there are more than 100 billion neurons in our brains. And remember, the young children you are working with have more of these types of brain cells than you do!

Neurons are made up of three parts: soma (cell body), axon (outbound projection), and dendrites (inbound feeders). Both the dendrites and the axons are specialized projections. Dendrites bring information to the cell body, and axons take information away from the cell body. Axons are long fibers extending from the neurons and carrying output in the form of electric impulses.

Information, in the form of an electrical impulse, flows from one neuron's axon to a synapse, which is a small gap separating neurons. As the electrical impulse reaches the synapse, it triggers release of a chemical neurotransmitter, which crosses the synapse and is received by other neurons' dendrites.

Dendrites form the major receiving part of neurons. The real work of the nervous system takes place within these highly complex, branching structures. The dendrites receive thousands of synaptic inputs from other neurons. But dendrites do more than simply collect and funnel these signals to the soma and axon; they shape and integrate the inputs in complex ways.

THE MYELINATION PROCESS

Learning is most effective when all the parts of the brain work together and the signals travel under good conditions along the various pathways. Myelination is a process that coats the neural fiber with a sheath, which fosters good conditions along the neural pathway. This process is one of the key reasons it is important for very young children to have well balanced diets and is the primary argument for why it is important for infants to drink whole milk for their first two years of life. The fat in whole milk works to lubricate the myelin sheath to allow the brain cell's impulses to travel faster. But certainly milk isn't the only source of fat. Diets rich in healthy fatty acids like omega-3 and omega-6 also work to coat the myelin sheath. If the fibers are not properly coated, they could become vulnerable and could cause disruptions in learning and behavior development.

THE PRUNING PROCESS

Scientists used to believe that over time if you haven't used those synaptic neuron cells, you'd lose them for good. This process, called pruning, occurs when the brain sheds unformed neurological connections. The greatest period of pruning was once believed to occur at the onset of puberty, although it also happens in several phases in the life span. Although we know this process removes unformed connections to make way for concrete thinking, new research suggests that new neuron cells can grow, at least in the hippocampus (Jensen 2008).

Furthermore, researchers are also finding that the development of the frontal cortex is nonlinear, meaning that the synaptic pruning and strengthening that occur in puberty are followed by a burst of synaptic growth throughout adolescence (Blakemore and Frith 2005).

Memory

When I teach workshops, I often start out by warning my students that I suffer from a rare disorder known as "Teflon brain." "Nothing sticks to my brain," I quip. "It just slips right off." In truth, memory is less of a skill and more of a process. There is no single location for all memory: this is why a person can have a great recall for specific dates in history but not be able to remember the capital of each state. I love history, and I can remember the stories about historic figures and their lives. But I can't tell you the date of the first Europeans arriving on Plymouth Rock or when wars were fought. I can usually recall *why* the wars were fought even though I can't remember the dates. That's because the reason (conquering land, fighting for freedom, etc.) has meaning for me.

Although it's best to think of memory as a process, there are several types of memory that have various functions:

- Short-term memory is the length of time we can hold small amounts of active, readily available information in our minds. Usually we can hold only seven chunks of information plus or minus two for twenty seconds (Miller 1956).

- Long-term memory occurs in the frontal lobe, where it is determined what information is retained. Information is sorted and sent to two categories—procedural memory or declarative memory. Procedural (how to do things) memory stores all the information related to how to do something like drive a car or tie your shoe. Declarative (facts that can be declared) memory is a collection of all conscious memories.

- It contains information that has been consistently repeated until it has become automatic.

- Automatic memory holds things you know automatically because of high frequency use, such as names, sounds, letters, etc.

- Episodic memory is when a prompt from automatic memory triggers another memory. For example, a few words of a song make you remember where you were the first time you heard it.

- Semantic memory holds information learned through words.

- Explicit memory is processed through the hippocampus and the cerebrum and describes the remembering of names, dates, facts, etc.

- Emotional memory stores positive and negative responses and brings up these responses if repeated.

- Working memory stores units of information for a certain period of time—usually only seven minutes. The difference between working memory and short-term memory is that working memory is storing units of information for the purpose of organization. Short-term memory is simply a holding place for a few seconds.

HOW MEMORIES ARE STORED

Actual memories are not stored as whole units in the brain. They are stored in bits and pieces throughout the various locations in the cerebral cortex. The smell and look of your new car are broken down and filed into different neurons. When you try to recall the day you got your first new car, you recall episodic memory. Then when you remember how it felt when your dad handed you the keys, your brain opens the emotional memory storage unit. When you trigger any of these sets of neurons, they wake up the adjoining neurons, and more memories can be unlocked and retrieved than what you had bargained for. Perhaps you also remember the first time you backed up into a telephone pole and your dad took the car away (Sousa 2006).

The more associations attached to a memory, the more complex the storage system can become. If a single memory can be stored in multiple storage units, the greater likelihood the memory can be recalled later with greater detail and accuracy. That would explain why memories are distributed fairly extensively throughout the cortex. It is as though the brain wants to "spread the risk" that if something happens to one part of the brain, the other parts will remain relatively unaffected. For example, memories of sound are stored in the auditory cortex, while memories of names, nouns, and pronouns are traced to the temporal lobe. Learned skills rely on the basal ganglia, while the hippocampus houses the episodic memory.

What I find interesting about memory is that it is *state dependent*: the brain stores memories based on emotions first. For children to have a positive memory about an event, their emotional needs have to be met. For example, when you read with a child, pick a comfortable place that is free from distractions that could interfere with your closeness. The child will remember the safe emotional feeling and will have a stronger memory of the interaction. Similarly, emotions conjure up memories that were retained while we were in that emotional state. Happy memories come back to us when we're happy, and sad memories come back to us when we're sad. If you want children to recall learning in positive ways, you need to create positive emotional states that will bind to their learning.

Our brain works equally hard when we are resting as it does when we are alert but not performing the same functions. When we are sleeping, our brain takes all the prior day's learning and decides which filing cabinet to store the information in. It sorts the information based on whether it is a procedural memory, such as a combination to a locker, or an episodic memory of an emotional experience. How embedded the memory is within the context of our learning determines where the final memory will be stored.

Because our memory storage cabinets are spread throughout the brain in different hemispheres, the best way we can ensure that an event, idea, or new skill reaches our long-term memory is to make sure we have encoded it by embedding multiple neural pathways.

Using music and songs is an excellent way to create multiple neural pathways to store information in long-term memory. Have you ever started to hum a song and from out of nowhere the words just appeared? The brain stores the words and music in different places, and certain triggers can pull out this stored information that seemed to have been forgotten. I can't remember what I had for lunch yesterday, but given the chance I could probably launch into my high school fight song. Set words to movement or music, and it will help children remember the information longer.

One of my mentors once told me to think about that old adage "Practice makes _____." She expected me to fill in the blank with "perfect." But she believed, and now I do as well, that what we are striving for isn't "perfect" but "permanent." Practice makes permanent! I am not interested in *perfect* children (I don't believe being perfect is their function), but I am concerned about helping them make *permanent* brain connections. It is only through repetition and extended opportunities to practice a new skill that new learning will make its way to long-term memory.

Unlike practice, which is the repetition of motor skills, the actual repetition and processing of information is referred to as "rehearsal" (Sousa 2006). Rehearsal is the continual reprocessing of information, which allows it to move from working memory to the long-term memory storage.

Considering there are so many different kinds of memory, it's important to do one thing in different ways to help ensure the memory gets caught somewhere along the line. Where it's stored and how it's retrieved depends on how important it is to you.

HOW INFORMATION IS RETRIEVED

How we retrieve information is affected by different factors, such as stress, anxiety, and conditions in the environment. John Medina wrote in *Brain Rules*, "You can improve your chances of remembering something if you reproduce the environment in which you first put it into your brain" (2008, 119). If you can't remember where you parked your car, you might be able to retrace your steps to help you figure it out. However, you'll have a harder time remembering where you parked if you're lost or you become stressed or anxious. When you're anxious, your adrenal gland releases a stress-induced chemical called cortisol, which mixes up the message being sent to your hippocampus. This makes it difficult to recall the memory with accuracy.

Memory processing typically requires three steps: encoding, storage, and retrieval. Encoding is the way in which memories are processed—through visual, acoustic, semantic, or tactile channels. We are able to remember something based on how it looks, how it sounds, what it means, or how it feels. If we can increase the channels through which a memory travels, we increase the chance that it will be stored and recalled more accurately.

The ability to create or re-create an environment where long-lasting memories are formed is vital to a child's development. What happens in the first few moments of learning cements the brain's ability to later remember what was learned. These first few moments create the code that becomes embedded in the memory and is responsible for which storage unit the memory will get sent to. The only way we can really tell if people remember something is by their ability to recall it (Medina 2008).

The whole point of brain-based learning is that the brain makes meaning out of experience and interaction. Each time a neuron is fired, it attaches to a network of more neurons that become wired together. These networks become stimulated by engagement with our environment, by our genes, and by biochemicals (Jensen 2008). The brain needs stimulation in meaningful and intentional ways to make those connections, and it needs prolonged engagement to ensure the formation of the neural networks. New content, to be truly "learned," must process through the brain at a micro level, then a macro level, and back to a micro level again. At each episode of engagement with the new content, through repeated exposure, the networks reconnect and compound to form concrete learning.

The learning activities detailed in chapter 4 are designed to be repeated and elaborated upon to help children create meaning and build skills needed for life and to help them truly use their full learning potential.

Creating Brain-Compatible Learning Environments

You've read about the parts of the brain, how they work, and what they do to make new information become knowledge (information that can be retrieved later when necessary). In this chapter, you'll learn how to create brain-rich learning environments. Whether you are a teacher, a caregiver, or a parent wanting to learn more about how to help young children develop, you need to recognize that the physical environment is critical when it comes to brain-based learning. The interactions between people and their environments are complex. For example, many early childhood educators think that an adult uses himself to improve the environment, while a child uses the environment to improve herself. Taking this a step further, Urie Bronfenbrenner (1917–2005), cofounder of Head Start and renowned American psychologist, developed the concept of bidirectionality. Bronfenbrenner examined the interaction between children and their environment. He theorized that the child affects the environment, and as a result the child is affected by the environment. Through bidirectionality he believed that for every action there is a reaction, and it is this back-and-forth process that allows learning to occur.

In an environment intentionally designed to provide brain-compatible experiences for children, the caregiver is available to children when they need guidance and assistance with new ideas. The teacher's role is to be on the sidelines, offering support when needed to help children develop new skills and facilitating interplay between children and the environment. The adult should never be the only source of input and exploration for children. A well-planned environment will provide children an array of learning experiences. When such an environment is combined with intentional, brain-based learning activities, children have the best of all possible worlds.

Constructing Meaning

We tend to relate better to new information if we have a way to connect to it. This is because relevance actually happens on a cellular level. When new input is sent to the brain, an existing neuron sends a signal to a nearby neuron to make a connection. If the connection doesn't carry an emotional tie to bind it to the neuron, it's not very likely to stick. If neurons aren't able to make connections, they're not likely to make what is being learned relevant. If they are able to make a connection, children interpret the new meaning and assimilate it into their learning schemas. Once a new meaningful connection is assimilated, children are then able to scaffold future learning on this knowledge.

Theorist Jean Piaget (1896–1980) suggested that children construct their own meaning from their previous knowledge and the world around them when they have an opportunity to engage in experiential, inductive hands-on learning. Placing children in an enriched environment and giving them repeated practice and further scaffolding of relevant information will strengthen that connection and help make the learning permanent.

Maslow's Hierarchy of Needs

In 1943 psychologist Abraham Maslow developed what he called a hierarchy of needs (see chart 2.1). A number of years after I first learned about this theory, I came to think of it in a brain-based way. Perhaps I'm a bit slow on the uptake, but when I began to look at the rungs on his ladder, I was able to think of this as a holistic approach to human development. Children need to have their needs met in order to be effective learners. Adults provide for the basic survival needs for children—food, water, shelter, and clothing. Only then can children move from basic survival mode to learning mode and so on up the hierarchy.

After basic survival mode, the second-lowest rung of Maslow's hierarchy is the premise that humans need to feel safe to thrive. Harsh comments by adults and even the use of sarcasm can threaten the emotional safety of children. When children are persistently exposed to threats in their environments, their brains' receptors adapt survival-oriented behavior (Jensen 1998). Children who come from homes filled with stress caused by violence or poverty can create defense mechanisms to protect themselves. Sadly, what they think is "protecting" them really leads to a disruptive learning environment, failure to develop personal relationships, and an inability to solve complex problems.

A brain-based learning environment must be free from stresses and threats to safety, but children also need to be able to predict events that will happen in their routines and not worry about being hurt or abandoned by the adults in their lives. A safe environment will clear the path for positive behavior and optimal learning performance. Presumably this will lead to feelings of love and belonging, which will lead to positive self-esteem and confidence and ultimately self-actualization. The higher the rung on the hierarchy, the higher the level of confidence, creativity, and ability to problem solve and accept the realization of facts.

Maslow's theory fits nicely with the holistic application of a brain-based learning environment that values positive social-emotional connections as a vital link to learning.

MASLOW'S HIERARCHY OF NEEDS

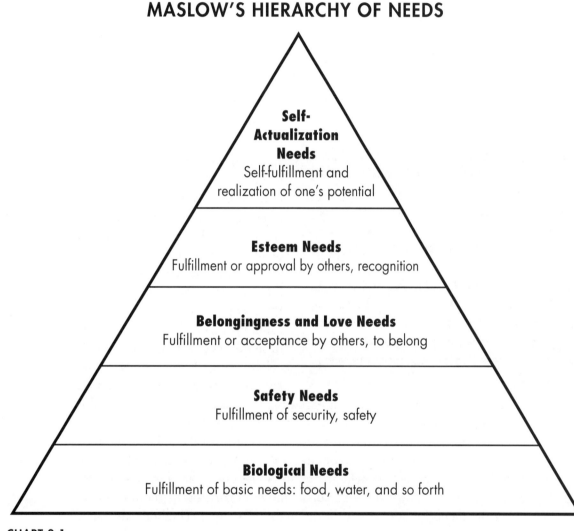

Self-Actualization Needs
Self-fulfillment and realization of one's potential

Esteem Needs
Fulfillment or approval by others, recognition

Belongingness and Love Needs
Fulfillment or acceptance by others, to belong

Safety Needs
Fulfillment of security, safety

Biological Needs
Fulfillment of basic needs: food, water, and so forth

CHART 2.1

Visual Input

The environment has a tremendous influence on the cognitive functions of the brain. Most of us derive the majority of our sensory input through the thalamus to our visual cortex, in the occipital lobe. Nearly 90 percent of all information absorbed by our brain is visual. In fact, our eyes are capable of registering nearly 36,000 visual messages an hour, with the retina accounting for 40 percent of all nerve fibers connected to the brain (Jensen 2008).

Knowing these facts should affect how we create visually stimulating—but not overly stimulating—environments for young children. The brain is wired to be drawn to novelty and to the use of images and movement. We remember better if we can touch and manipulate concrete visuals.

COLOR

Colors such as yellow, beige, and off-white are optimal colors for learning. Brighter colors like red, orange, and bright yellow trigger energy and creativity, while using greens and blues can create feelings of calm and tranquillity.

Using the color red to write a list can spark creativity when brainstorming (Shiller 1999).

We tend to think that early learning environments need to be splashed with every color of the rainbow to stimulate the brain. How many Fortune 500 board rooms have rainbow-painted walls complete with plastic furniture in matching hues? I haven't been to any, but I would bet at least a buck fifty that there are not very many. What colors do they use to create calm, nurturing environments that promote cooperation and critical thinking? When posters, text, pictures, and other wall hangings are displayed against a neutral backdrop, the contrast between the color change will stimulate the visual cortex by adding novelty (Jensen 2008).

> **Think about this...**
>
> Recently I heard that teachers have been discouraged from using a red pen to mark grades on papers because it is believed that seeing the grade in red triggers a negative reaction even if the score isn't necessarily low.
>
> I lack the conviction of a preference or the empirical data to suggest what is actually right here. But it is worth noting that children will respond to color in direct relationship to how it is used. Although purple is the new red for many teachers who do not want to invoke harshness when grading children's work, red is associated with energy and creativity and may be the spark a young learner needs to see how to improve his work.

That doesn't mean that off-whites and beiges are the only colors to be used. You can use vibrant colors to create a change in space or function. Soft cool colors such as light greens and blues encourage feelings of calm and comfort. Using different colors in different parts of the room will help set the mood for how you want the brain to respond. The brain responds best to movement, contrast, and novelty.

TELEVISION

Many caregivers, parents, teachers, and child care providers have come to believe that television is "evil." Jokingly referred to as the "idiot box" by some people, television is still a staple in child care programs and homes with young children. The argument against television watching does have merit in a brain-based setting. It is vital to a young child's development to limit his television watching. Images on the TV screen are two-dimensional, but the brain learns best in three dimensions (Jensen 1998). When we can physically touch something, the brain is able to have an "aha moment" when it really connects. Television robs children of those moments, and over time the repetition of two-dimensional images short-circuits the brain.

Olfactory Stimulation

If you are a fan of the sitcom *Friends*, you might remember the song Phoebe created about a smelly cat. Even though I couldn't actually smell the cat during the episode, I could relate. I had, in fact, smelled a smelly cat before, and even the thought of the scent caused me to have a negative physical reaction. But in thinking about pets and smells, the episode also reminded me about the time I once said about my beagle, "Casey smells like a dog." Without skipping a beat, my

Although I certainly don't advocate for every kid to have her own fifty-two-inch plasma television, sometimes television can provide the contrast and stimulation that reach certain types of learners.

I have worked with an autistic child who wasn't comfortable with groups of people around her. She became quite agitated when other children would surround her or when an adult would attempt to make eye contact or try to engage her in activities. However, she loved the television and was quite drawn in by a video of a soft-spoken teacher introducing sign language. The video's combination of music and movement, visual contrast, and novelty encouraged this child's verbal expression, and she would follow along with the voice prompts of the teacher in the video. For this child, the two-dimensional world was less threatening, and she responded enthusiastically to the use of television.

That is not to say we left her alone in this two-dimensional world by herself. I was there to follow along with dance movements, I provided feedback on how she was doing learning the signs, and I used sign language throughout the day. I repeated phrases the teacher used in the video, and I used the music to engage her in three-dimensional activities. A good teacher uses all available technology and materials to effectively reach the different learners in his classroom.

then four-year-old daughter Elyse said, "She *is* a dog." I was so happy about Elyse's observation that I still remember that interaction.

Using scents in the environment, such as peppermint, basil, lemon, cinnamon, and rosemary, can improve mental alertness. Lavender, chamomile, orange, and rose are known to calm nerves and promote relaxation (Jensen 2008). Color and scents often can go hand in hand—or eye to nose. Well, I think you get the idea here. If you use the color yellow for a reading corner, try putting a basket of lemons there to create a richer sensory experience.

Using scents in an environment can stimulate the olfactory gland to generate a positive connection with the nervous system. Olfactory regions provide triggers for endorphins, which regulate feelings of pleasure. Smells are underused in the environment to create mental alertness, feelings of calm, and relaxation. Be mindful of allergies or irritants that could bother young children's eyes and respiratory system. If fresh flowers cause sneezing, they are best kept outside.

Movement

It has been proven that movement keeps not only our bodies healthy but our brains healthy, as well (Jensen 1998). Exercise causes the release of brain-derived neurotrophic factor also called BDNF, which improves cognition by boosting communication between neurons. If exercise improves learning and memory, we could reason that a lack of activity can lead to depression and lack of retention. Glucose, which is a type of sugar produced from carbohydrates, is the fuel the brain uses to keep the body moving and to stay alert. Despite our desire to give ourselves a glucose jolt with some caffeinated beverage or sugary sweets, this type of sugar only creates a temporary boost that leads to a crash. But the high created from movement will keep the brain supplied with glucose and powered up longer.

Exercise helps the brain in several ways. Movement improves circulation, so the heart pumps more oxygen into the brain, allowing more oxygen and nutrients to travel to the neurons. When the brain has more oxygen, it performs better, is more alert, and is generally fired up! Gross-motor repetitive movement causes the release of dopamine, a mood-enhancing neurotransmitter (the stimulus that excites neurons) from the hypothalamus. Sedentary activities limit the dopamine. With less dopamine in our bloodstream, we are more likely to be in a bad mood. If movement is rigorous enough to be considered aerobic, our bodies are able to trigger adrenaline-noradrenaline responses that help us face challenges. The greatest benefit, however, is that exercise actually grows new brain cells and prolongs the survival of existing cells (Jensen 2008).

For children to get exercise in your environment, allow enough physical space for gross-motor movement indoors without obstructions. You don't need a huge amount of space to give a child what she needs to get her wiggles out. A safe area free from obstructions (even if you have to move something out of the way for a time) works best. If possible, create the opportunity for a variety of movements. For example, I have a platform with two steps children climb and then jump off onto a tumble mat. Children use a giant ball to roll and bounce on. This also helps them develop balance.

MUSIC

Music has many practical applications in brain-based learning. Music promotes socialization, triggers memories, gets children up and moving around, and also calms children and helps them wind down. Music does so much for our brains—from improving our mood to physically changing our brain chemistry. It is one of the best brain-based learning tools we have at our disposal.

When music reaches the ear, it travels as an electrical impulse to the thalamus, located next to the auditory cortex. From there the auditory cortex routes the music to different regions of the brain. For example, if you introduce new concepts to music, followed up with hands-on sensory exploration of individual math counters, the brain is able to retrieve this learning from multiple places in the future, which strengthens the chance for long-term memory. Studies have found that when children have formal music instruction, higher-functioning regions of the frontal lobe, which is responsible for logic and mathematics, are stimulated (Sousa 2006).

Music can prime the brain for specific, focused learning and can be used to deliver content embedded in the music. Researchers discovered that when music instruction was given to children under the age of seven, their corpus callosa were actually larger and thicker than those of children who had not had the same musical exposure (Strickland 2001). This is important because the corpus callosum sends signals back and forth between both hemispheres. A denser corpus callosum increases the signal exchange, making the interaction quicker and more elaborate.

Incorporating music into curriculum, whether brain-based or otherwise, is so important that books have been published containing lists of songs to use for specific learning. In Eric Jensen's book *Top Tunes for Teaching* (2005), he lists seven reasons music should be part of every curriculum:

1. It's assessable; you can assess the merit of musical learning.

2. It's brain-based; music has a biological basis and reaches many parts of the brain.

3. It's culturally vital, improving social skills and cross-cultural connections.

4. It has no significant downside; no known study links failure to perform with music.

5. It has survival value, helping transmit culture from one generation to the next.

6. It's inclusive, breaking down barriers across demographic strata.

7. It's wide ranging, including a variety of genres and skills.

Music can trigger emotions, stirred through the release of the brain's natural hormones. Music can create emotional states of mind and can increase social contact when listeners achieve a relaxed mental state. Most effective is how music can be used for recall. Think about the alphabet song or the cleanup song sung by a purple dinosaur. You can sing this in your sleep, right? So can the children in your program, even if they don't realize it. Music can penetrate the subconscious. Do you ever get a song stuck in your head? That's what I'm talking about. A song swirls around in our brain until it finds a resting place in a memory storage unit and stays there until we need to recall it again.

Sometimes that song might be in a box in a corner of my brain covered with cobwebs, but it's still there. When I had the good fortune to meet Peter Yarrow of the group Peter, Paul, and Mary at the 2008 National Association for Family Child Care Conference in Chicago, Peter asked me if I thought our group was through with hearing him sing "Puff the Magic Dragon."

"Oh no!" I exclaimed. "This group will never tire of hearing that song." Even if we haven't heard it sung in decades, I am certain that little Jackie Paper lives within all child care providers. And so it was that Peter Yarrow took the stage, and for his grand finale he sang "Puff the Magic Dragon" and invited the audience members up to sing with him. The room felt lopsided, with most people either on the stage or huddling close to sing a favorite childhood song with a legend.

Novelty

When I teach a brain-based learning workshop, I always attach my name tag upside down. Inevitably half of the class will comment to me that my name tag is upside-down. Usually they say something like, "Hey, did you know your name was upside-down?" And I'll say, "Yes, but I also know that the brain craves novelty." And later in the workshop I describe how my upside-down name tag can provide stimulation for our brains.

"It's like this," I say: "If my name tag hadn't been turned upside down, you would have just smiled at me and walked in and taken your seat. But because my name tag was upside-down, many of you made a point of approaching me from across the room. Your own brain had to recognize that these letters weren't right side up and wondered, *Is that really a name or something else?* You had to make eye contact and open your mouth to say, 'Hey, your name tag is upside-down,' and you were genuinely concerned about my well-being, assuming that I would be more comfortable if my tag were right side up. That is a lot of stimulation for the brain compared with 'Hey, look, that's a name tag,' and you then just go take your seat."

Creating an environment where children have the chance to experience novelty in action is a lot of fun. In my classroom I rotate pictures so that children can look at them from a different angle and experience a different perspective. The brain responds to the newness with increased neural activity, building the networks and connections in a positive way. The growth tapers off, though, as the newness wears off.

In your efforts to add novelty, I gingerly caution you not to stray too far from conventional routine, because young children also crave routine for comfort and security. So while I don't advocate having the routine be so jumbled up that children become stressed, I do strongly encourage you to keep them guessing about just what it is that you are going to change. An example of this is not to change solid routines, meaning the order in which you typically do things, but change how you engage in the routine. For example, we go to the playground daily at 10:30 AM, and that doesn't change unless the weather prohibits it. Some days, though, instead of walking to the playground, we skip. Maybe on the way back we won't skip, but instead we'll hop on one foot. The brain has to keep guessing what's coming next. The novelty keeps it primed and ready at a moment's notice.

Environments with too many predictable features tend to reduce the neural activity in the brain. When the environment is challenging, a child's brain will continue to make new and more concrete connections. When we get used to certain patterns in our environment, we become less challenged.

I remember my days of learning to drive. My instructor told me that roadways are not made directly straight for extremely long distances, whenever possible, because the lack of change in the terrain will cause the driver to become inattentive. The road must, to some degree, continue to be a challenge to stimulate the driver's brain. If I am driving and I feel sleepy, the best way to jolt my brain is to take a very swift glance out the side window. Even that brief break in the visual trance created by my attentiveness to the road resets my brain's clock for the length of time it can adequately pay attention.

Creating novelty in the environment is not the same thing as creating competing stimuli. Novelty isn't about creating a three-ring circus but about looking at the same thing through a different lens, perhaps a kaleidoscope sometimes or a magnifying glass at other times. Remember to focus on one thing at a time, even though the lens through which you examine it might change.

What is not a good idea is to look at two (or more) things through the same lens at the same time. When teaching children new skills, it is best to present each new activity with a break in between. It is not effective to teach two related skills in the same learning block. This is one time when trying to get two birds with one stone doesn't work. Despite the long-held notion that some people are better at multitasking than others, the truth is that the brain can only attend to one thing at a time. Sure, it can go about the business of doing several things at once, but it won't be giving any one activity 100 percent of its attention.

It's important to have a break between learning two similar types of physical activities so as not to confuse the neural pathway. Breaks for the brain are crucial in allowing it time to optimally sort and retain information in ways that will make it easy to retrieve later on. Trying to teach a child how to play golf and baseball in the same day will not result in creating a "Tiger Ruth." As the brain learns a new skill, the motor cortex works with the cerebellum to create pathways that pull together the movements necessary to perform the skill (Sousa 2006). If a child is introduced to a second activity that is very similar to the first before the motor cortex has finished making its connection, chances are pretty good that this child will not excel in either sport as a result of his brain getting the circuits crossed.

Whether for motor skills or cognitive concepts, the brain needs between four and twelve hours to process learning and to cement the pathways necessary for each new thing learned. Without the time to process and practice each skill separately, the brain will not be able to change structurally, which makes the skill permanent (Sousa 2006). Work on one thing at a time if it's important that the skill really sticks.

My Favorite Things

A stimulating intentional learning environment can offer children many opportunities to make permanent connections. Here are a few of my favorite things in my environment.

BOOKS, BOOKS, AND MORE BOOKS

Always be sure to have lots of books in each environment. Books are multifaceted and multipurpose. They tell stories, create imagery, promote vocabulary, provide instruction on how to do something, and depict people and places and things from around the globe. They connect us, inspire us, and entertain us.

PUZZLES

Puzzles are great brain builders because they help develop the ability to reason and deduce, sequence, problem solve, and develop logical thought processes. Puzzles work to stimulate hand-eye coordination and develop a sense of spatial awareness.

SWINGS

Install a swing with a low seat back (securely anchored to a ceiling beam). It will provide stimulation to the vestibular region of the inner ear, which leads to language development. Encourage language and literacy engagement with children while they are in the swing to capitalize on brain stimulation. Children can swing while being read to, drawing, or looking at picture books. The swing also promotes gross-motor development and novelty by bringing the outdoors in. Children don't expect to see a swing inside. Make sure that the swing is low enough for children to get into it on their own and that there is proper ground protection in case of falls.

LOOKING UP

My good buddy Jeff A. Johnson (coauthor of *Do-It-Yourself Early Learning* and author of *Everyday Early Learning* as well as family child care provider extraordinaire) convinced me to install an eye hook in my ceiling. What perfect sense this makes. When children have to look up, it changes their visual perceptions and sends a new signal to the brain to create a different pathway. We use lots of things with our eye hook; one of our favorites is a pulley. The children use a bucket to raise and lower items so they can try out cause and effect. We explore the questions "What happens if we let go of the rope?" and "What happens if we put in something really heavy?" and others. The children use their gross-motor skills to pull the weight of the bucket when it's full and their brains to make predictions about what is going to happen.

We don't stop with the pulley. We have multiple points in the ceiling with hooks for zip lines, clotheslines, temporary art displays, and curtain dividers. We even once suspended a parachute from the hooks to create a rainforest canopy. If you use hooks, be careful to securely fasten objects that will hang above children, and place protective cushioning on the floor if necessary.

FLOOR PLAY

Too few children have the opportunity to freely explore without restriction. Just look in any baby catalog, and you will find hundreds of items designed to hold an infant upright and confined for long periods of time—bouncy seats, saucers designed for exercising, and vibrating contraptions of all shapes and sizes. I can only imagine what they will come up with next. As a caregiver of young children, I don't discount the helpfulness of a swing to soothe an infant when I have many other children to care for, but I take issue with props that restrict an infant's ability to freely explore her natural world.

In 1960 an average two-year-old spent an estimated two hundred hours in a car over the course of a year. Today the average is five hundred hours strapped in a car seat. Hundreds of hours of critical motor development have been lost. A direct benefit of motor development is the stimulation received by the vestibular region of the inner ear. This region plays a key role in school readiness. Infants given periods of vestibular stimulation by rocking gain weight faster and develop hearing and vision earlier. Dyslexia is also connected to lack of vestibular stimulation (Jensen 1998).

Because the brain relies on multisensory input to create concrete pathways, try to create as much sensory stimuli in the environment as possible. Consider using various textures on the floor that children can feel in bare feet or crawlers can experience. You don't need to drastically recover your floors, but subtle changes in texture, such as smooth, cool surfaces including marble or tile, wood flooring, and different piles of carpet, can create different sensory experiences for children. These different floor surfaces also create a variety of "terrains" for floor play. Cars move better on smooth surfaces, and you have to work harder to get a ball to roll on plush carpet. Every surface can be a learning tool if it's intentionally put to good use.

DRAMA QUEENS AND KINGS

Dramatic play helps children rehearse their newly acquired knowledge and put this learning into cultural and social context. Props, such as hats, coats, aprons, profession-based implements (safe tools for doctors, teachers, mechanics, etc.), help children learn within a social context. They get to try on new roles and see how they fit. What is it like to be a mommy or a daddy? Can girls be mail carriers, and can boys be nurses? Children need to explore social situations through play to gain skills they'll need when the situations become real.

OUTSIDE IN

I love to use baby pools inside year-round. Sometimes I put pillows in the pool, and we "dive into reading" and use it in our reading corner. Other times we put the slide over the end of the pool, and the children slide into a pool full of rice. Children love how the texture tickles their feet. They try to see if they can keep the ball spinning around the edge of the pool (thus learning about centrifugal force). Pools, swings, slides, large scooters, and ride-in child cars are all things you would normally see outside. We bring all those things inside to create novelty and enhance children's understanding of the physical world.

Don't forget to add plants and flowers and natural materials such as wood to enhance your environment. Always check to make sure plants and flowers are nontoxic and that wood surfaces are free from sharp edges and splinters.

INSIDE OUT

Kitchen play centers are staples of indoor play, so why not include them outside? Set up a station where children can "cook" and prepare meals. You'll be amazed at how many scrumptious meals they can make out of mulch, twigs, chunks of grass, and a bunch of objects you can't really identify.

Give children the chance to read books outside. Many people only think to read to children or give children books inside because they don't want the books to get damaged. But if you have taught children to take care of the books and you are mindful of their placement, reading books outside can add a tremendous amount of sensory input.

Art activities are a natural for outside, so make sure to bring outside paper, paint, chalk, and basically anything you can use to create art.

Is It All Necessary?

When conducting workshops about how to help early childhood educators create brain-compatible environments for children, providers bring up the point that all this hard work is quickly undone when a child enters grade school. "Not necessarily" is my answer. Sure, when a child has had the opportunity to learn and explore in a brain-based learning environment, it can be a shock to enter grade school, where the teacher may lack knowledge about and willingness to use brain-based learning in the classroom. It can be a difficult transition for the child to go from having the freedom to explore his environment to being required to sit at a desk and be quiet. But the inherent benefit of early exposure to brain-based learning makes it worthwhile.

We know that most learning patterns are set by age five, so it is crucial that the early environment is maximized to get the most out of this critical time. Our job is to set the stage, provide the props, offer the comfort and personalized care each child needs, and then step back and watch the magic unfold.

Practice

Putting Theory into Practice

Now that you have a better understanding of the structure and function of the brain and how to create a brain-friendly environment, I'll discuss strategies to help cement neural connections. These new connections will create networks that develop over time as the brain has prolonged and repeated exposure to new information in a variety of ways. These strategies will add tools to your brain-based learning tool kit.

This chapter will cover a broad range of strategies aimed at putting theory into practice. It discusses the power of play, motivation and rewards, executive function, scaffolding, the Zone of Proximal Development, relationships, social context, emotional intelligence, critical thinking, and the importance of language and literacy. Having these learning strategies in our tool kits as caregivers and teachers is essential in being able to help children develop their own tool kits.

In their book *Tools of the Mind: The Vygotskian Approach to Early Childhood Education*, Elena Bodrova and Deborah J. Leong (2007) discuss the importance of helping children develop mental tools to do things beyond their natural abilities. These mental tools include ways to increase memory so that children can expand the amount of information they are able to recall. What is most notable about this approach is that the actual development of these tools changes the way in which we think, attend, and remember beyond our natural ability.

If children don't learn how to use these mental tools, however, they will not become intentional learners (Bodrova and Leong 2007). If they cannot focus their minds in purposeful ways, their learning is inefficient. Often when stimuli are presented randomly, children only learn how to be reactive learners instead of active learners. These children are unable to self-regulate or direct their own learning. The goal of helping children develop tools is to ensure that while adults cannot always control the way in which stimuli are presented, they can help children learn how to self-regulate and respond appropriately to those stimuli in meaningful ways.

The Power of Play

Play is a child's work (Paley 2004). It is how children construct their own meaning and learning. I remember sitting in an early childhood education advisory board meeting with a group of educators lamenting about the pressures introduced by No Child Left Behind. A woman I greatly respect and admire, who is a curriculum specialist for a public school, remarked, "You know, I am waiting for the day, probably twenty years from now, when I'll open the newspaper and there will be a big headline: 'New Research Shows Play Is Good for Children'!" We all laughed a knowing laugh tinged with regret that today's children are being shortchanged by the pressure to achieve on an "academic" level earlier and earlier.

Playtime should be sacred in childhood. It's when children get to practice all the things they need to make permanent. It is not *their* language development time if I am the one doing all of the talking. I talk a lot, so I have lots of practice. Playtime is when the children get to practice. Free play enables a child the best opportunity to practice critical-thinking, problem-solving, and imagination skills. Life skills are learned and honed in the dramatic play area, and opportunities to practice those skills arise every day through self-selected learning activities.

The brain needs practice to cement those neural pathways to help make what is learned permanent, and nothing does that better than a child constructing or reconstructing the environment in which this learning takes place. Play is not a break from instruction. I repeat: Play is not taking a rest from the real work of learning. Play *is* the real work of learning.

In *The Play's the Thing: Teachers' Roles in Children's Play*, Elizabeth Jones and Gretchen Reynolds (1992) cite Piaget's words, "To understand is to invent." The only real way for children to do this is to have opportunities to construct their own knowledge by having hands-on interaction with the physical world and with other children.

It is interesting to note that when Jones and Reynolds observed children playing "school," children played teachers who acted stern, gave directions, and enforced rules. It would appear that even very young children see teachers as the "givers" of knowledge. But knowledge is not for the teachers to give. The children must experience it for themselves for it to be meaningful.

What Is Fair?

The greatest joy that brain-based learning offers children is the thrill of learning for learning's sake. Usually when children are intrinsically motivated to learn more on their own, they are typically greater risk takers. I don't mean they want to jump out of moving cars, but they will be the ones to jump up and say, "Let me try!" It's this kind of motivation that we want all learners to possess.

In the long run, it is believed that rewards do very little to motivate underachievers and in many cases do more harm than good (Jensen 2008). What is more helpful for all learners is to replace material rewards with positive alternatives, such as enhanced privileges, more control, and extended choices for creativity.

As children get older, the problem with rewards and motivation is the realization that life isn't fair. Have you ever wondered exactly what being fair means? I know what fair doesn't mean. It is not about giving each person the same thing. That might be *equal*, but when you are being *fair*, you are giving each person what he needs. The following anecdote illustrates this point.

You're sitting in a restaurant eating dinner when you begin to choke on a piece of sirloin. Your dinner partner jumps up and calls out, "Is there a doctor in the house? My friend is choking!" A doctor gets up and comes over and assesses that yes, in fact you are choking and that you would benefit by her performing the Heimlich maneuver. She turns to the other patrons in the restaurant and says, "This woman needs me to perform the Heimlich maneuver on her, but I don't want to be unfair to all of you, so please stand up and form a line over here to the right so that I can perform the same procedure on everyone."

"That's absurd," your friend says. "No one else needs the procedure but her!"

"Yes, that is true," says the doctor, "but if I do it for her, according to the fair treatment of all restaurant diners, I have to do it for everyone else. Please step to the right so we can begin."

Meanwhile you've passed out from a lack of oxygen, and the other diners are throwing up their house salads. Fair doesn't mean giving each person the same thing. It means giving each person what is right for her. When put that way, don't you think it's better to give only the person who is choking the Heimlich maneuver?

The trend these days seems to focus on the model of childhood equity that "equal" means "fair." As a parent of three children and as a family child care provider, I know better. I know that I can't set equal standards for each of my children, because they are all different ages and have different capabilities. I know what is developmentally and physically appropriate for each of my children. One shouldn't have to do something (or not do something) just because the other child gets to and vice versa. It's not about what's equal, and sometimes it isn't even about what's fair. Every person is unique, and life doesn't always have to be fair to be right.

In an enriched learning environment, a child should have all of the elements necessary to stimulate his emotional, physical, and mental well-being. This includes providing challenge and novelty to help each child develop fully. If a child learns that if another child gets a toy he should have the same toy also, he isn't learning how to use his resourcefulness to find another toy to play with. He won't learn to occupy his time while he waits for the toy he desires.

Demanding that a three-year-old share his toy just because another child suddenly demands it is not being fair to the child who had the toy to begin with. Just because another child decides she wants to play with the car doesn't mean the child who has that car is finished. Many adults feel it is okay to ask the first child to share because it's teaching empathy and a willingness to be kind. But in fact it's sending a message that his feelings matter less than the second child's does. What's wrong with asking the second child to wait or helping her develop an interest in something else? Each teachable moment doesn't have to include every single child involved in the moment. Sometimes the lesson being learned today is only for child number two, and maybe tomorrow child number one will have the chance to benefit from the lesson. "Even" doesn't equal "fair." Everybody will eventually get a chance to play with that toy even if that chance doesn't happen today. A child's ability to process what is fair is affected by his level of executive function. The more chances he has to experience when fair works for him or against him, the better he will become at being able to problem solve. We want him to be able to ask, "If I didn't get the toy this time, what can I do differently next time so that I can get it?"

Executive Function

As mentioned in chapter 1, the prefrontal cortex is responsible for the executive functioning of the brain. Highly developed executive function allows individuals to be good decision makers, organize their thoughts, control impulses, assess risk, and think critically (Caine, Caine, McClintic, and Klimek 2009). Ultimately it is these skills that help children develop their mental tool kits, which in turn become lifelong learning skills.

Executive functions include

- regulating emotions
- having a sense of the future and its relationship to present behavior
- engaging working memory
- problem solving and developing resourcefulness
- developing creativity and critical-thinking skills
- being aware of and able to reflect on self-critical consciousness

Children who have well-developed executive function are able to use hindsight as a way of guiding present or future decision making. As a result they are able to have foresight and insight into self.

It is believed that children who have strong executive function

- are able to set goals they believe they can attain;
- can self-regulate;
- are positive and optimistic;
- have good social skills and the ability to get along well with a variety of people;
- are independent;
- can problem solve and be resourceful;
- succeed under a degree of pressure;
- have good time-management skills.

Helping children develop these skills is critical to their ability to succeed in life. When children are able to construct their own learning from their experiences within a supportive and nurturing environment, they develop competence and confidence to learn and do more (Caine, Caine, McClintic, and Klimek 2009).

According to Eric Jensen, "Learning changes the brain because it can rewire itself with each new stimulation, experience, and behavior" (2005, 13). The windows of optimal learning only close a bit; they don't ever shut completely. Children (and adults) continue to possess the ability to learn new information. We should never think that an opportunity to learn something new has passed. You *can* teach an old dog new tricks.

Various approaches should be used to engage children in intentionally designed brain-based learning activities, because, as we've discovered, there are many ways people learn as individuals. What is appealing to me may not be as interesting to you. As Howard Gardner's theory shows, every person has multiple intelligences, which simply means we all learn about things in different ways.

Children need many opportunities to try things in different ways not only because they learn in different ways but because they need to strengthen the neural connections associated with the new skill. The brain has very specific routes it wants information to travel to ensure storage in long-term memory. If we want things to get stuck there (and we do!), we need to make sure we've given the brain many chances to learn what it is we are trying to teach it.

In my multiage classroom I have made accommodations for children who are learning at different rates. Adapting my curriculum to be appropriate for multiple ages enables children to self-regulate their interests. Some children who are learning faster can move on to more sophisticated materials, and others can slow down and work at a pace they find comfortable.

Scaffolding

The theory of scaffolding was developed in the 1950s by Jerome Bruner, a cognitive psychologist, to explain the interaction when an adult helps a child complete a task that is beyond the child's current ability (Bodrova and Leong 2007). By providing structure, resources, and support, the adult helps the child construct new knowledge based on previous learning. As mentioned earlier, scaffolding is closely linked to the Zone of Proximal Development, in which the novice learner is able to advance to a higher level of performance with the help of an adult or more skilled person. Over time as the scaffolding builds, the level of help necessary to complete a task, for example, will decrease as the child's skill increases. As children gain new skills, it is imperative that we continue to present them with increasingly complex challenges to further expand on those skills. This scaffolding helps the brain form multiple pathways. Thus, the skill becomes permanent, and the child is able to recall it more easily.

Zone of Proximal Development

One of psychologist Lev Vygotsky's key theories, the Zone of Proximal Development (ZPD), is directly linked to the development of executive function. The ZPD is created by what a child can do by himself and what he can do with help. It's important to know that the ZPD is not static; it changes as a child learns a new skill. The lower end of the zone is what a child can do independently, and the top is what she can do with assistance. The goal is to increase the difficulty of the task so that the child can attain higher levels of thinking and deeper knowledge. Support provided by a more competent child or an adult can include things such as giving hints or clues, restating the question, asking new questions, or even demonstrating the task and walking the child through it step by step. This help can also come from indirect contact, such as setting up an environment that allows the child to practice a certain skill or set of skills.

In effect the ZPD becomes a construction zone: the place where children are able to construct meaning from their prior learning (Bodrova and Leong 2007, 48). The way in which they are able to recall their prior learning is the direct result of brain-based learning. If ZPD is effective, a child will be able to extract knowledge to further her understanding of new information.

To demonstrate the effectiveness of the zone, I use a strategy known as "Ask three before me." This strategy is designed to motivate a child who is having difficulty with something to ask his peers for help before asking for help from an adult. I don't use this strategy because I'd rather not be bothered to help the child in need. In fact, I am really using another one of my favorite strategies during this time: "Learn, do, teach."

When a child learns to do something, "the thing" is introduced as an idea. Then if the child is allowed to do "the thing," the idea begins to form a neural connection. When a child then turns around and teaches another child "the thing," the connection is made.

If a six-year-old child came to me and said, "Ms. Nikki, can you tie my shoe?" I'd say, "Yes, I can. I've had a lot of practice, and now it's easy for me." He'd then ask again if I could tie his shoe for him, and I would reply, "No. I'm not the one who needs the practice. But Josh needs the practice. He's only been tying his shoe for three months. Why don't you ask Josh if he can show you how to tie your shoe?"

If a child has to ask three friends how to tie his shoe before he comes to me, chances are pretty good that at least one child will get some practice tying a shoe. It gives the child who is being asked to help the opportunity to teach the skill, thus cementing the learning. It also helps the child who is asking for help work on his ZPD. Eventually it will expand enough that he will be able to do most things on his own and in turn become a teacher to others. This ultimately will contribute to his self-confidence and ability to self-regulate his emotions.

Relationships

It cannot be said enough that the most critical element of any early childhood setting is the relationship between the adult and the child. Safe emotional connections set the tone for everything else. Relationships are the foundation on which everything else is built. Remember that the brain remembers emotional memories first. Adults have an inherent responsibility to create the most emotionally secure learning environments possible.

According to Lise Eliot, it appears that attachment is programmed into limbic system development (2000). The need to remain close to an adult is so strong, in fact, that infants instinctively know how to use certain techniques to signal their desire for close proximity to their caregiver. They cry, coo, smile—they do whatever they have to do to make sure they have the attention of their caregiver.

As the frontal lobe develops and a child becomes more independent, the attachment becomes stronger (Eliot 2000). At about the time a child can crawl away from her caregiver, she begins to worry about her reconnection with this adult and may experience what is know as separation anxiety.

As long as a child is receiving consistent, loving, responsive contact from parents and caregivers, she will be able to develop a healthy limbic system necessary for strong social and emotional development. But if a child experiences stress and elevated cortisol (stress hormone), the components of the limbic system (hippocampus and amygdala) will become damaged. The longer the levels remain elevated, the more damage is caused. Caregivers who are playful, friendly, and sensitive can reduce the chance that the cortisol levels will rise during their contact (Eliot 2000).

Social Context

According to Vygotsky, social context is central to how children construct meaning from their own learning. A great deal of what children learn is culturally generated (Bodrova and Leong 2007). Vygotsky believed that everything a child learns is rooted in her culture, both present and past. The cultural history of our ancestors influences not only what we know but how we come to know it.

When constructing a classroom with all of the necessary components for brain-based learning, it is important to remember this ancestral history. While the brain needs many things to build long-lasting meaning, such as an environment free from threats with an abundance of emotional security, it also needs opportunities to self-regulate. The process of developing executive function is culturally based, and while the environment plays a key role, the social context for learning is paramount.

While it's true that we are more alike than different, the fact still remains that we are different, and there is much to be learned from our diversity. We have different skin colors, and our facial features come in different shapes. We are different in our values and beliefs because of our national heritage, our socioeconomic status, our affiliation with political parties, and our religions, not to mention our various physical, emotional, and mental abilities. This is the social context each person operates in.

When my husband and I decided to open our hearts and our home to children to offer family child care, we asked ourselves, "What if parents don't come?" We thought that if they didn't come, we would never know if it was because of the color of our skin or because of the type of program we offered. Fortunately for us, they did come, and as far as we know, our skin tones have not stopped families from choosing our home for quality child care.

I realize now that these early thoughts were based on my own bias about how I thought other people behaved when it came to racial diversity. I was influenced by old stereotypes in assuming I knew how parents in my community would react to placing their children in the home of an interracial couple with multiracial children. I know now that I was wrong.

We teach children to classify things in order to make sense. I remember one conversation I had with a mom during our annual program picnic about how wonderful it is that our children have embraced each other's differences. The mom said, "You know, I think it's wonderful that the children don't even notice their differences—it's like it doesn't even matter." I thought carefully about my response before I spoke, because I didn't want to perpetuate any more stereotypes. But I also felt strongly that she wasn't exactly on target. Children do notice differences, and it does matter.

My understanding about how people come to form stereotypes led me to believe that what she was saying is that the children don't notice that some of them will be judged based on their skin color and that it's nice that the children can accept each other for who they are.

While I can appreciate her remarks as being positive, I don't believe they are correct. Children do notice differences. As educators we spend a great deal of time teaching children to discriminate between objects and classify them into a category that they can make sense of. What is missing is the definition of the meaning of discrimination. We are not teaching children to negatively single out people and make judgments about what those differences mean.

The reason we teach children to look for differences is to help them make connections—brain connections. We teach them how to discriminate among colors and shapes and objects so they can form neurological patterns that store this new information in a way that can be retrieved later on. By learning to classify each object within their mental schema, children can draw from this knowledge as they scaffold new concepts and form concrete thinking patterns.

What we are not doing is burdening our children with damaging baggage that tells them that differences are bad. But at the same time we should recognize that we can't treat every single person exactly the same—which is not to say we can treat any one person less than another, but we should respond to each person as an individual.

I remember one day a kindergartner in my program looked as though she had been crying. When I asked her what happened, she told me that at school the teacher was doing an "all about me" activity in which she wanted each child to take two pieces of paper that had been precut into the shapes of little hands. Tia carefully selected two hands a slight shade of pink for her project. When the teacher noticed this, she immediately came over to Tia and said, "No dear, you need this color of hands," and she gave Tia two brown hands.

Tia explained that she looked at the paper hands and then at her own hands again and decided she really wanted the pink hands. When she went to exchange the paper, the teacher insisted she keep the brown hands. Tia held out her hands to me palm side up and said, "See, my hands are pink!" It's too bad her teacher didn't accept Tia's decision to depict her hands as she saw them. One side was brown, but the other side was pink. There is always more than one way to see the same thing—it's all how you look at it. But more important, it was critical to allow Tia the freedom to make her own choices about her project and her self-image.

AVOID THE TOURIST APPROACH

Discovering new ideas can be exciting, but caution should be used with multicultural exploration. Be clear that the process of discovery is happening *within* each child. Christopher Columbus didn't discover America, after all. The continent was already here when he happened upon it. Help children learn that discovery happens within them. It's what happens when the brain makes connections, and not something that comes into being just because the children are learning about it for the first time (Derman-Sparks 1989).

But by all means, make the journey. Explore and discover to your heart's content. But try to avoid taking the tourist approach. This means you don't just celebrate Dr. Martin Luther King Jr. during February, which is Black History Month. You don't just teach about Native Americans during November because of Thanksgiving. In *Connecting Kids: Exploring Diversity Together* (Hill 2001), author Linda Hill describes what she calls "an inclusive tour guide" as a person who helps children find ways to integrate activities and interests and find common ground. Hill explains that children learn by watching and listening. Competent tour guides take children into the heart of diversity by modeling genuine interest in different people and subjects, asking questions about what is important to all children and learning about their unique home lives. Learning must be presented within the context of what children already know. Even when presenting new ideas that may counter the currently held beliefs, a brain-based approach is going to start with what is known and present new ways of thinking about it.

Let's say I want to talk about different types of homes people live in around the world. I start by asking children what they know about this subject. If I learn that children believe that all people in Africa live in grass and mud huts, I need to make sure I am able to show them (or let them experience for themselves if possible) that some people in remote villages might live in huts, but most cities have brick and wood houses like we do. If I only let the children make models of grass and mud huts and don't support their learning about how not all people live in these kinds of houses, I would be using the tourist approach. If I invite a guest in to talk to us about his home in Ghana and bring pictures, videos, or other art to visually present the children with facts to counter their original idea, I am taking the tour guide approach.

INCLUSIVE LEARNING

Some children have special needs and special requirements for their care, but all children need and deserve healthy environments in which to thrive. As our early care and education system becomes more sophisticated and comprehensive, parents and children are reaping the rewards of quality inclusive care.

Understanding that each person is unique allows an endless opportunity to create diverse learning environments. With careful planning, providers are able to design an environment that incorporates quality early learning standards but can also promote inclusion. A provider who includes adaptive materials and maintains a supply of varied materials for creating art projects, imaginative play, and experiential hands-on learning specifically for children with special needs will be creating a learning environment that can help all children learn how to appreciate diversity.

A brain-based learning environment is naturally adaptable to be an inclusive environment if designed well. A brain-based learning environment should be able to provide opportunities for children with varying learning styles so children who develop differently will have similar opportunities appropriate for their developmental and physical needs. Brain-based learning encourages repeated exposure to new ideas and skills presented both in distinctly different ways and in similar ways. And providing prolonged exposure to new skills, which is a function of brain-based learning, is extremely helpful for children who may have processing or cognitive delays or behavioral disorders requiring repeated rehearsal in practicing new skills.

Emotional Intelligence

There is an old story about a man who was walking along a river when he noticed a person floating downstream. He immediately jumped in and dragged the person to safety. Before too long, another person came floating downstream, and another, and another, until the man was frantically pulling people from the river. In no time at all, other passersby came to help, and they set up a triage center. Then they built a large hospital to treat all the people who had been pulled from the river. These were all well-meaning gestures in an effort to help the people who had the misfortune of finding themselves in trouble.

One day a man happened upon this scene and asked why all these people were floating in the river. The team was very busy hauling people from the water and didn't have time to answer. They said, "Jump in and help us save them." The man observed the scene and then began to walk upstream. Not satisfied with merely helping pull people from the river, he was determined to find out what was causing the people to fall in. Eventually the man found the problem. A storm had caused a bridge to be washed out, and no one had put up a warning or a fence to keep people from driving off the road and into the river. The man immediately built a barrier along the river, added bright warning signs, and redirected traffic away from the river. And thus people stopped falling into the river.

What does this parable have to do with social-emotional development? We can teach our children problem-solving skills that can help them avoid the pitfalls of life. We can teach them not just to be sympathetic but to be empathetic and engaged in the lives of those around them. Which would you prefer: a fence at the top of the river or a hospital at the bottom?

Much of our emotional intelligence is learned in the first year, but it is within childhood and adolescence that we settle into the emotional habits that will remain with us the rest of our lives (Goleman 1995). If Daniel Goleman is right, and current thinking believes he is, emotional intelligence is vital to human development, and it begins in infancy.

The brain stores emotional memory first, so it would stand to reason that by being emotionally intelligent, we have the potential to create lasting memories about the things we learn. The self-awareness created by learning how to be emotionally intelligent heightens a child's ability to learn to recognize his own feelings and eventually to manage his emotions in constructive ways. Self-control is achieved by delaying gratification, resisting impulsive urges, and developing deep and meaningful relationships.

Developing emotional intelligence requires repeated opportunities to practice in order to strengthen the neural pathways to the brain. Modeling prosocial behavior with young children is a good place to start the practice. Or rather, think of it as a rehearsal—like in a play. Help children become players in the theater of positive behavior complete with a curtain call and encore! Developing strong social-emotional skills takes practice—getting it right and getting it wrong. Even the best teacher can't set up a teachable moment about how another child will react to someone's bad behavior. Sometimes those things have to work themselves out on their own. If one child is repeatedly telling other children he doesn't want to play with them, and then one day when he asks if he can play with the group, they rebuke him, this creates the opportunity to help the child reflect on the actions of his behavior. As you can imagine, this is a long and arduous process, because we can't allow negative and hurtful behavior to go unchecked. But we can let some natural consequences run their course so that children can learn lasting lessons.

Visual Patterning

Ever walk into a room and wonder what you came in there for? If you return to the place you last were when you thought to go into the other room, you might recall what it was you were looking for. When it comes to memory, thoughts, words, and images can linger in the mind long after the event has past. When you lose your keys, what is the first thing you do? I close my eyes and try to remember where I was when I had them last. I try to picture everything I can about that moment.

The brain looks for patterns to make meaning and is constantly looking for similarities in our environment. We are more likely to remember something if we have seen it before (Medina 2008). Draw attention to this fact when working with young children to help them practice visualizing something they have seen before: "Remember last week at the farm we saw the cows?" This can help recall the memory with more accuracy and link this memory with new details.

Critical Thinking

It's hard to imagine that by simply observing the people around them, children can understand their world. But it's true. Children learn a great deal about behavior—what is important to us as adults and what is important to each other—by simply watching what is going on around them. In turn, they discover they can re-create these same experiences in a way that is meaningful to them.

Let me give you an example. One four-year-old named Will noticed I was making notes on a clipboard about what I was observing. I use these notes to assess the progress of the children and to document their behavior.

When Will noticed that I would watch the children and then write someting down on the clipboard, he got a clipboard with a sheet of paper and assumed a position of observation. I noticed him looking specifically at the same child I was observing. My attention shifted from the other child to Will because I was curious about what he was going to do next.

After a few moments, he announced he was finished. I asked him what it was he had been doing, and he said, "I was looking at Kevin to see if he was going to build a house."

I asked, "So did Kevin build a house?"

Will replied, "No, Kevin never builds houses with blocks."

I asked Will, "If Kevin never builds houses, why did you think he would build one today?"

His response was, "I really wanted to play houses with him."

Will understands connections. He couldn't tell you he's making connections, but he came to his own conclusion about why observing was important. He was interested in playing house with Kevin and wanted to see if Kevin shared his interest. It is through this kind of observation that I can actually see brain connections occurring. To see the lightbulb going on above those little brains means children are developing critical-thinking skills and developing their own learning strategies.

There are a variety of ways to help children develop critical-thinking skills, but one of my personal favorites is a method of inquiry known as KWL. A provider will have the chance to ask children what they know (K) about a topic, what they want to learn about a topic (W), and finally what they learned about the topic (L). As children take an in-depth look at subjects that interest them, they are able to construct their own learning about the subject they are exploring. One positive effect is the rich brain experience they undergo during this process.

I remember the first time my father came to stay with us for an extended period of time. He hadn't been around young children for a long time, probably since I was a young child myself. A child would ask me a question, such as, "Ms. Nikki, why are there always worms on the ground after it rains?" My response would be, "That's an excellent question. Why do you think there are worms on the ground after it rains?"

"Ms. Nikki, how many apples would I have if you gave me three more than the two I already have?"

"I don't know, Kevin. Let's count them together."

My father, probably thinking I really didn't know the answers, began to respond to the children's questions with direct answers. I didn't want to stifle his involvement, but I really wanted him to challenge the children to think more about these questions without just handing them the answers. I finally had to explain to him that I wasn't answering the questions because it's a strategy to get the children to think for themselves. He let out a sigh and said, "Oh, what a relief. I was beginning to think that college education was all for nothing!"

Asking questions that require yes or no answers does little to promote brain-based learning. While these types of questions seek identification or confirmation, they severely limit discussion. Open-ended questions, by contrast, create active involvement and stimulate thinking. Questions can be subjective (those that contain a reference that could be different for each person) or objective (those that contain a reference that would be similar for each person). They can also be open-ended or closed. Here are a couple of examples:

Subjective: What makes your lines different from those marks?

Objective: What makes this house different from that barn?

Open-ended: Tell me what you were thinking when you drew this picture.

Closed: Did you draw a house?

Subjective: On a scale from one to ten, rate how much you liked lunch.

Objective: Tell me three things we had for lunch.

Open-ended: Tell me about lunch.

Closed: Did you eat a sandwich for lunch?

Invite children to make predictions, think critically, and express themselves with enriched vocabulary. Make it a habit to add questioning to your routine. Marilyn Matthews, one of my favorite mentors, would ask children each day, "Where are you going to go?" and then she would wait for their answer. Then she would ask, "What are you going to do when you get there?" She believed this helped them develop a plan in their mind about where they were going to go and to have goals for what they wanted to accomplish once they got there.

Follow-up questions after the exploration time could include, "So, Brandon, you went to the block center to build a high-rise building. Did you build the high-rise?" Brandon might then explain that he had wanted to, but when he got there, he discovered that all the long rectangular blocks were no longer available, so he had to make a low strip mall instead. (Marilyn's students would have used those exact words, because she modeled that vocabulary for them.) This kind of inquiry demonstrates that children are capable of having plans and can use critical-thinking skills to reshape their plans when roadblocks arise. It's all a part of well-developed executive functioning.

Convergent and Divergent Thinking

Convergent thinking brings ideas together and makes things simpler. Divergent thinking creates challenges and makes things more difficult. We need to create learning environments that constantly challenge children, providing tasks that become increasingly more difficult to help children expand their skills (Jones and Cooper 2006). Asking divergent and convergent questions gives children the opportunity to formulate ideas that link theory and require interpretation.

Convergent questions are usually asking for the recall of certain facts or of how to do something to determine the person's prior knowledge. Answers to these types of questions will generally be right or wrong.

Example: "Tell me what shapes you used to build this house."

Divergent questions are best used to get children thinking and solving problems. These types of questions have many correct answers, and sometimes the answers are unknown.

Example: "Why did you decide to build a house?"

Both convergent and divergent questions are helpful in determining what children already know and how they are learning, but divergent questions, which allow for more open-ended thought and critical thinking, help children construct more meaning from this knowledge as a result of their own experience.

Language and Literacy

The frontal lobe of the left hemisphere is where language is processed, primarily in Broca's area and Wernicke's area, which are the two major processing centers in the brain. The visual cortex, which processes visual stimuli, such as written words, is located at the back of the brain across both hemispheres (Sousa 2006).

According to David A. Sousa, one of the most extraordinary things about our brain is the ability to learn spoken language (Sousa 2005). All human beings have the ability to learn all of the distinct sounds of all languages on the planet. As we learn the language of these sounds, we add meaning and are able to express our thoughts and emotions.

While all humans will develop spoken language (providing there isn't a barrier such as a disability or a lack of exposure to language), neuroscientists discovered early on that boys and girls process language in different ways. Boys tend to process language in the left hemisphere, and girls tend to process language in both hemispheres. Scientists were able to observe that girls had a much larger and thicker bundle of neurons (corpus callosum) connecting both hemispheres (Sousa 2005). It is this observation that led researchers to explain how girls develop language earlier and more quickly than boys.

Nevertheless, if there is a lack of exposure to language, young children will not develop the cells in the auditory cortex. In order to develop the nuances of pronunciation and larger vocabularies, children as young as six months old need to be read to.

Language and literacy skills are already being developed at birth. Everything you do to help foster a child's growth and development can be connected with language and literacy, and it all starts with reading. Helping children to learn the meaning of words isn't the same as simply knowing what a word is (Sousa 2006). Words are symbols. Repeated exposure to written, oral, and sign language helps children make connections about the meanings of these symbols.

SIGN LANGUAGE

Humans are designed to be communicators. Infants seem eager to communicate with us the minute they can breathe on their own. "Hey, who turned on the lights? Why is it cold? When do I get to get back in the womb?" All this is heard in the form of a child's first scream following her delivery. From then on the cries seem to mean similar things: "I'm hungry, I'm stinky, I'm cold, I'm hot, I'm tired." How can we tell what she means if all her cries sound the same? Even though her vocal system hasn't fully developed, by around six months she can use basic sign language to communicate her needs.

Linda Acredolo and Susan Goodwyn conducted a longitudinal study funded by the National Institutes of Child Health and Human Development that showed hearing infants who use symbolic gestures understood more words, had larger vocabularies, and engaged in more complex play than children who did not use sign (Goodwyn, Acredolo, and Brown 2000). Parents of these hearing children whose babies used sign to communicate noted a decrease in frustration and an increase in communication along with enriched parent-child bonding.

Because 90 percent of what we take in is through visual processing, sign language is an excellent way to help young children express themselves visually while creating novelty. With more than thirty specialized areas of the visual cortex, linking with neighboring neurons can create more than twenty linkages.

RECEPTIVE AND EXPRESSIVE LANGUAGE

Language is processed in the frontal lobe of the left hemisphere, where verbal information is processed into receptive and expressive language. Receptive language is the comprehension of information by understanding words and sounds, and it begins to develop at birth. Within months a newborn can tell the difference between a happy voice and an angry voice (based on tone, cadence, and volume). Language skills do not automatically improve as a child ages; intentional effort is required to stimulate language development as the child grows.

Expressive language is language and gestures used to communicate meaning. Around a year of age, children begin to demonstrate their use of expressive language, depending on what exposure they have had to spoken language. They learn expressive language by hearing speech, grammatical forms, syntax (sentence structures), pragmatics (meaning of the sentence depending on how and where it's used), and rhythm.

Children need to be read to often and given the opportunity to explore the written and spoken word. Modeling the behavior of a reader and reading with children can lay the groundwork for a lifetime of literacy success. Sharing personal stories not only creates an oral history through generations but helps children develop their own personal narrative. The more you include words and reading in children's daily lives, the better readers they will grow up to be.

My Grandmother's Stories
Every single evening, before I go to bed,
My grandma tells me stories that come out of her head.
She tells me many stories about relatives she knew,
And what's best about her stories is that all of them are true.

She tells me about her mother who knew Martin Luther King
And followed him on a freedom walk on a beautiful
    day in spring.
She tells me about her children and the great things
    they have done.
She put them all through college, every single one.

When Grandma tells me stories, I listen very well.
She has such wondrous things to say, so many things to tell.
And when she tells me stories, her voice is like a song.
It makes me feel all warm inside. I know where I belong.
(Bardige and Segal 2005)

Through spoken language and dramatic play, children have the opportunity to develop both receptive and expressive language. An excellent way to practice expressive and receptive language is through songs and rhymes.

Rhyming
In the book *Reading Magic: Why Reading Aloud to Our Children Will Change Their Lives Forever* (Fox 2001), Mem Fox laments how depressing it is that many children today come to school without even a basic ability to recite

rhymes. She implores us to get songs and rhymes stuck in the minds of children at a very early age.

Rhyming activates different parts of the auditory cortex in the right hemisphere. And if children tap out a rhythm, they activate the left frontal cortex, left parietal cortex, and right cerebellum (Tramo 2001). This is how rhyming and movement work together to get more parts of the brain firing at the same time, building stronger neural networks.

The Words of a Song
Some words stick on the tip of my tongue
Like the words of a song that I have never sung.
And if those words would just fall out,
You would know what I'm singing about.

I sang with the chickadees just this spring.
They always love the songs I sing.
And if my tongue would get out of my way,
I could keep singing songs all day.

(Bardige and Segal 2005)

The Primacy/Recency Effect

Before I wrap up this chapter, I want to briefly introduce a concept known as primacy/recency. Because of the way our brains work, we are usually only able to remember the first and the last thing we hear or see of material presented but not much in between.

Try to name the first president of the United States. Easy, right? What about the current president of the United States. Easy again, right? Now, without searching online, can you name the eighth president? How about the twenty-fourth? Probably not. Chances are pretty good that you immediately thought of President Lincoln, even though you might not have known that he was the sixteenth president. Big events help us remember details that we might not otherwise remember. Lincoln was a big deal. Other names you may have remembered are Kennedy, Reagan, and Bush. (By the way, Martin Van Buren was the eighth president, and Grover Cleveland was the twenty-fourth.)

One key thing to note about the primacy/recency effect is that the clock the brain uses resets after a two-minute break. So for about every ten minutes of instruction, you need to give about two minutes of rest time. One great instructor I had used a line I love to recycle: "The brain cannot absorb what the butt cannot endure." This reminds me to have my students get up and get moving as frequently as possible. But it also reminds me that

I have to follow the ten/two rule to make sure that the brain doesn't forget all the good stuff sandwiched in between the first and the last thing I said.

The two-minute break rule is usually used as a transition time or prep time, but it gives little brains the time they need to sort out new learning into the memory filing system.

When you introduce new ideas to children, it's important to repeat the information in many different ways to make sure you don't always leave the good stuff in the middle. If we know that the brain remembers the first thing and last thing it hears, then we need to switch up the order in which we present the material next time so the brain has another chance to make that connection permanent.

Because our brains apply the primacy/recency effect whether we like it or not, it's important that we are mindful of the position of emphasis that we place on specific information.

I hope you've enjoyed learning about the theory behind brain-based learning. Now it's time to make some permanent connections with fun learning activities. Take a break. Stretch your legs. Get a drink of water. Rest your brain a bit before you head into chapter 4. I don't want you to miss anything.

Brain-Based Learning Activities

I think I became interested in brain development by studying my favorite expert in the field, Dr. Seuss. I believed him when he told me I had "brains in my head" (Seuss 1990). And here I am helping to create fun brain-based learning activities for young children.

Crossing the Hemispheres

While each activity in this chapter provides fun ways to learn in a brain-based way, there are a few things you can do with children to help "prime" their brains before you begin. These activities are called "cross laterals," and they are designed to open up both hemispheres of the brain and get each side talking to one another.

Simple exercises such as writing your name in the air with your elbow or doing the "Macarena" are cross laterals. The act of taking your arms and crossing your body sends a signal that says, "Hey, left brain, this is right brain—are you awake? I think we're on!"

Let's Make It Permanent!

As I wrote in chapter 1, practice makes permanent. It's finally time to rehearse some of these great brain-building strategies I've been talking about. You have learned how to create brain-compatible environments and how to use various tools to encourage brain-based learning, and now it's time to really get down to it. I've separated the learning activities into eight different categories:

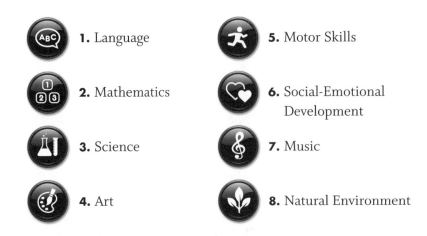

1. Language

2. Mathematics

3. Science

4. Art

5. Motor Skills

6. Social-Emotional Development

7. Music

8. Natural Environment

To provide children with truly brain-compatible learning opportunities, all of the activities within any one category can really apply to multiple categories. To help clarify how the activities are connected, logographic symbols at the top of each activity indicate the different categories related to each activity.

Each activity is broken into sections to help you with lesson planning. Each activity includes

- the targeted age of children doing the activity;
- a list of materials;
- what brain connections are being supported;
- multisensory variations to make each experience richer;
- diversity adaptations to create multicultural experiences.

You probably won't be surprised to see that each activity has ways to extend it on the same theme. As I've emphasized throughout the book, it takes repeated opportunities to try the same activity to make the connection permanent. So be sure to try out the many different ways you can do each activity and adapt it for different ages. This way you can provide the novelty that the brain craves so much and extended learning opportunities to help cement those connections.

I have purposely chosen these activities to promote critical thinking, deductive reasoning, and gross-motor opportunities to engage the brain through a variety of avenues, such as music and movement. To help you customize the activities for different learning styles, I have also included activities with multiple intelligence opportunities.

Working with Infants

The activities detailed in this chapter address the learning needs of children from eighteen months through schoolager. Because of the specific needs of infants, learning activities for them look different. To help you understand how to create brain-based learning activities for infants, ideas are provided in the introduction to each of the activity sections. Think of infancy as the introductory phase for all types of learning. Continue to present new ideas, and reinforce previously presented ideas to lay the foundation for future learning. The journey of a thousand miles begins with one step.

Making Connections Last

Creating rich brain-based activities involves extended periods of time connecting and reconnecting ideas. Projects that take time to evolve give children opportunities to problem solve, work as a team, and use divergent thinking. While short episodic activities are still critical to providing novelty and an engaging way to build new ideas, longer projects create ongoing opportunities to cement concepts in long-term memory.

You've made it this far—that's quite an accomplishment. As beloved performer and educator Dr. Jean Feldman says, "Kiss your brain!" Every time a child makes a good choice or solves a problem, encourage her by saying, "Kiss your brain!" (Feldman 2009).

Now let's get ready to grow those brains!

LANGUAGE

Brain Connections

Language is processed in the frontal lobe in the brain's left hemisphere. When you combine language with creativity from the right hemisphere, you create permanent connections in the whole brain.

In a brain-based learning environment, we are counting on children bringing what they know to the experience and building on that knowledge. With language, as with everything else, we are welcoming what the children bring to the learning process.

In her book *Poems to Learn to Read By: Building Literacy with Love,* my dear friend Betty S. Bardige and her mother, Marilyn M. Segal, discuss the concept of "outside-in" language development (Bardige and Segal 2005, 166). Inside-out language development focuses on words and how to translate the sound from the printed word. Outside-in represents what children know outside of the printed word that supports their understanding of the printed word. When children learn language from the outside-in rather than the inside-out, they are able to bring learning context to the actual meanings of words.

Typically children learn "concrete" words first: an example of outside-in learning. Concrete words are those that already have meaning to a child. When a child brings prior learning to something new, he is more able to make it stick.

Supporting Language in the Environment

Be as creative as you possibly can when providing language support in the environment. Everything you include will be used by children to build their language and literacy skills, so choose wisely. Below is a list of some ways to support language in the environment. Feel free to add your own ideas. I recommend *Lessons for Literacy: Promoting Preschool Success* (Hansen and Hansen 2009) as an excellent resource for environmental language ideas. Label as many concrete things in the environment as possible. Incorporate environmental print in dramatic play, blocks, and reading centers by stocking the area with

- clipboards with paper and pencils (can be used in restaurant play, for shopping lists, etc.);
- menus from real restaurants (imitate real life, can demonstrate diversity by using a variety of cultural food choices);
- cereal and other real food boxes (connect child to real-world environment, provide font-rich literacy, and can demonstrate diversity by using a variety of cultural food choices);
- real cans of unopened soup and other items (provide a deeper sensory experience and build muscle and fine-motor control).

Language and Infants

Every activity that you do with infants should be rich with language. Infants' auditory receptors are wide open as they experience the new and exciting world unfolding right before their ears. Infants can hear a wide range of sounds that may not be audible to adults. By experimenting with a variety of noises, you may be offering infants more sounds than you realize, giving infants the opportunity to develop their auditory discrimination skills. Keep a running narrative during your interaction with infants to offer a rich variety of language. "Eli is reaching for that ball. He is stretching out his arm. Eli touched the ball. Does Eli like the ball? What is Eli going to do with the ball?"

Read, read, read, read, and read. Reading to infants (and all children) has tremendous lifelong benefits. This cannot be emphasized enough. For starters, when you read to an infant, you typically hold him or sit very close. This closeness is the beginning of a beautiful friendship. You are starting to build trust with him. You should limit the amount of time you read to just a few minutes, but you can also encourage the baby to touch the book and look at the pictures to round out the sensory experience.

Selecting Books to Support Language

When you are selecting books, it's important to be intentional about the titles you include. Consider choosing books that have won Caldecott, Newbery, or other awards, but also take your cues from children. Do books with colorful illustrations get your child's interest? Does the story engage your child or hold his interest? Does the book have familiar objects, places, or people that children can relate to? Does it present new ideas that can expand thinking on subjects children have some familiarity with? Do the books discuss topics that support families' moral beliefs? Do the books promote prosocial messages? If the books excite you and make you want to share the stories enthusiastically with young children, chances are pretty good they'll like it too.

Make sure that young children have a choice of books that are not too heavy on text. Older children may prefer more text and fewer illustrations.

Choose books that avoid stereotypes of people based on gender, age, ability, and race. Instead, look for and select books that realistically represent all people, and especially look for books that represent the families in your program. We want children to be able to relate to books that have familiar objects, places, and people in them. But we also want them to learn about people, places, and objects that are not like them. Inviting books open up this new world to children and help them make new connections.

And last but not least, the books you choose should be pleasurable to read over and over and over again. Remember practice makes ___? Answer: permanent. Right!

SUGGESTED BOOKS—AGES BIRTH TO FOUR

Arnold, Tedd. 2000. *Parts*. New York: Puffin Books.

———. 2003. *More parts*. New York: Puffin Books.

Hennessy, B. G. 1992. *Jake baked the cake*. Pictures by Mary Morgan. New York: Puffin Books.

Sierra, Judy, and Barney Salzberg. 2004. *There's a zoo in room 22*. Orlando: Harcourt Books.

SUGGESTED BOOKS—AGES FIVE TO EIGHT

Cronin, Doreen. 2000. *Click, clack, moo: Cows that type*. Pictures by Betsy Lewin. New York: Simon & Schuster.

———. 2004. *Duck for president*. Illustrated by Betsy Lewin. New York: Simon & Schuster.

Finchler, Judy. 2003. *Testing Miss Malarkey*. Illustrations by Kevin O'Malley. New York: Walker & Co.

Thaler, Mike. 1998. *The cafeteria lady from the Black Lagoon*. Pictures by Jared Lee. New York: Scholastic.

My Favorite Story!

Intended Ages

two years and older

Brain Connections

creativity, expressive and receptive language, divergent thinking

Materials Needed

- a journal, sketchbook, or other hard-bound book with blank pages

  or

- make your own with blank paper and staples along the spine

  or

- use a three-ring notebook

My favorite story is always changing—it's never the same story twice. In fact, there are no words written on the pages of this book. I found a book at a local bookstore that was bound like a hardback book but had blank pages. I started out by telling the children I was going to read them a new story. I began to turn the pages and "read" the story. I had to explain that there weren't any pictures in the book, but they could create the pictures in their minds. After I was done with the story, I showed them the book so they could see that the pages were blank.

The children soon caught on that this was a fun way to create stories, and every time I read the story, it had a different beginning, middle, and end. All children feel successful when they "read" this book, because there are no actual words. It can be whatever they want it to be.

Use the blank book as a prop to hold while you make up a story. If you need help coming up with story ideas, think about favorite stories you read to children and make up different characters or different endings.

Extension Activities

After you tell one of your favorite stories, children can re-create the story in a book they will make themselves. Give children sheets of paper (heavy card stock is best) and provide a variety of materials to help them write and illustrate their pages. Once children are finished creating the pages for their books, you can laminate the pages to make them sturdier, or use a three-ring binder with page sleeves so that you can change and add pages later. You can also use a report cover to protect the pages so children can take their books home or add them to a portfolio. Continue adding these books to your library.

Multisensory Explorations

Use different material to make the books, such as a quilt book made out of fabric or other types of materials.

Diversity Adaptations

Help children understand the value of passing on oral language traditions. Literature is available about how the oral traditions of cultures around the world, including African American, Creole, American Indian, Hispanic, and Asian cultures, ensure that stories not written down anywhere are passed through the generations. Sharing these storytelling techniques with young children is a language-rich learning experience.

What Came First?

Intended Ages

three years and older

Brain Connections

sequencing, receptive and expressive language, predicting

Materials Needed

- different pictures of a story mounted on heavy card stock

Sequencing is a skill needed for reading as well as math and science. Children need to get the hang of what comes first, what comes in the middle, and what comes last. A fun way to practice this skill is to let children construct their own stories by putting the pages of the story together.

Create pages with pictures on them showing a stage of a story. For example, for the story of "The Three Little Pigs," you might have pictures of pigs building houses, a wolf blowing down two of the houses, and two pigs running to the third pig's house. Place the pictures on a table and let the children take turns putting the pages in the order of the story.

Extension Activities

You can use storyboards of traditional stories, but you can also make up your own stories that can have different endings based on how the children place the cards in order.

Multisensory Explorations

The cards can be made with textured paper, cloth, or scents. To allow children to self-correct, you could number the cards on the back to allow the children to check if they got it right.

Diversity Adaptations

Use stories with characters from different cultures. Use pictures of real people, and try to avoid stereotypes.

Alpha Box

Intended Ages

three years and older

Brain Connections

sensorimotor, problem solving, expressive and receptive language

Materials Needed

- twenty-six different bins (use recycled baby wipe boxes with large openings for little hands to reach inside)
- items that represent each letter of the alphabet (e.g., bean bags, buttons, bells)
- letters (use large sturdy letters like those found in wooden puzzles or foam sets)

I remember the first time I made alpha boxes. I went to a dollar store and bought twenty-six plastic shoe boxes with lids. The cashier said, "Boy, you have a lot of shoes!" I said, "Yes, one for each letter of the alphabet." She gave me a quizzical look, and I just smiled.

Keeping items that start with each letter of the alphabet in a separate box will help children become familiar with a variety of objects that relate to the letter. This helps with word recognition and beginning and ending sounds.

Let children play with related objects and practice making the letter sound, writing the letter shape, etc. Frequently change the items in the box.

Extension Activities

Have children go on a scavenger hunt to find the alphabet objects to put in the box. Label items and their placement on shelves to grow vocabulary.

Multisensory Explorations

Use a variety of materials with different textures so children can distinguish the shapes and objects.

Diversity Adaptations

Use objects that reflect materials found in children's homes. Label items in English and another language, such as one spoken by children in your program.

Magic Writing

Intended Ages

two years and older

Brain Connections

sensorimotor skills, expressive and receptive language

Materials Needed

- three cups of yellow cornmeal or sand (more or less depending on how many children will be working at a time)
- one cookie sheet or other tray per child
- visual prompts

A fun way to get prewriters accustomed to using an object to create shapes is to let children practice using their fingers to make letters or other shapes in cornmeal (or sand) on a cookie sheet. Think of this as a tactile Etch-a-Sketch.

To create the writing surface, place cornmeal or sand on a cookie sheet or other tray with a lip to prevent spillage. Model for children how use a finger to write letters in the cornmeal or sand.

Use visual prompts, such as cards or pictures, or put the cards on the bottom of the tray under the cornmeal and have them trace the letter through the grains.

If the children make a mistake, no problem—just give the tray a jiggle to smooth the grains, and they can start over.

Extension Activities

Other objects can be used to make the shapes, such as a pencil, a stick, or even cookie or play-dough cutters.

Multisensory Explorations

For more sensory connections, allow children to use a substance with a different texture to write in with their fingers. You can use finger-paint or pudding to practice writing skills.

Diversity Adaptations

Use substances distinct to various cultures, such as different kinds of flour, grains, dirt, or sand.

Sensory Scribbles

Intended Ages

two years and older

Brain Connections

sensorimotor skills, expressive and receptive language, predicting

Materials Needed

- letter or shape prompts

We often use our hands to identify the feel of a shape, but what about our arms or our backs? A new way to help the brain recognize shapes is by allowing a different surface on the body to experience the touch and sensation of a shape. Do these surfaces send the same signal to our brains?

Have children sit one behind the other, and have one child draw a shape using her finger on the other child's back. Ask the other child to guess what shape was drawn. Then have them switch to give the other child a turn at drawing.

Extension Activities

If children can't think of the shapes on their own to draw, use cards with shapes or letters on them as prompts to help the child remember, and then show the other child what the shape looked like.

Multisensory Explorations

Use different objects to draw the letters besides just a finger. Try a paintbrush or feather duster.

Diversity Adaptations

Be respectful of a child's preference (or family's culture) regarding touching. In addition, be aware of any children who might have sensory integration challenges, making touch uncomfortable for the child.

Bag o' Wonder

Intended Ages

three years and older

Brain Connections

predicting, divergent thinking, memory

Materials Needed

- pillowcase
- various objects of different shapes, sizes, weights, and textures

Children are curious by nature. What am I saying? So are adults. Don't we all want to know "What's in the bag?" Let's find out with our bag o' wonder!

Place various objects in a pillowcase, and have children reach in and guess what it is they feel. Have them describe what they are feeling before they pull the item out to see what it is.

Extension Activities

Have children create theme bags. Each bag has items related to one another, and the children take turns guessing what the theme of the bag is. For example, a bag containing rocks and plastic dinosaurs could be a prehistoric theme bag.

Multisensory Explorations

Vary the objects to be multisensory: hard, soft, prickly, smooth, squishy, etc.

Diversity Adaptations

Create themes representing the children in the program. For example, if a child has a parent who is a plumber, the theme bag could have small PVC pipes, a wrench, and a small plunger. This might provide opportunity for greater recall, because the child might have seen her parent with these items.

Rhyming Scavenger Hunt

Intended Ages

four years and older

Brain Connections

divergent thinking, receptive and expressive language, critical thinking

Materials Needed

- objects with names that rhyme (coat, boat, goat)
- paper
- pencils

I love rhymes. In fact, I challenge children to talk in rhyme whenever possible. It can be a hard thing to get the hang of, but it sure lends itself to funny words!

> Rhyming is a tricky thing.
> You never know just what to bring.
> You might need a ribbon
> Or a goat
> But never a flibbon
> Or a shmoat.
> —Nikki Darling-Kuria

My favorite part of rhyming is the giggles it produces.

Introduce rhyming words by reading classic nursery rhymes to children. Have children go on a scavenger hunt to find items that rhyme. They can check the objects off a list. Make a chart with pictures so nonreaders can identify the object and place a mark next to it. Or they can collect the objects and bring them back to the circle.

Extension Activities

Make up new rhymes from the objects collected. Write them in a book or on a large piece of paper to display in the room. The older the children, the more complex the rhyme should be. Ask them to come up with a rhyme using the names of all the objects they find and tell it to the group.

Multisensory Explorations

Use materials with various textures, weights, and colors.

Diversity Adaptations

Use rhyming words that stretch vocabulary, including words in other languages.

flannel fantasy

Intended Ages

two years and older

Brain Connections

expressive and receptive language, fine-motor skills, creative thinking, sensorimotor skills

Materials Needed

- felt material to make objects that represent the story
- Velcro if you need to attach felt pieces
- flannel-covered board to display

Flannelboards are an excellent way to enhance storytelling by providing a rich sensorial experience. This tactile activity will help children tell their own stories as well as other stories they are familiar with. Even very young children can tell stories using these felt pieces. They can create the story by moving the pieces around, and an adult or another child (think Zone of Proximal Development) can use his voice to tell the story. Even toddlers realize they have played a role in making the story come to life.

Provide children with a flannel surface to use felt pieces on. The board can be mounted on the wall or placed on a table or an easel. I suggest multiple boards for multiple children to work simultaneously. The pieces used for the board can vary in many ways, but be sure to use larger pieces for toddlers.

Extension Activities

Pieces can be laminated to make them more resistant to wear from toddlers. Velcro can be used to attach the flannel pieces on the board. Make stories using pictures of the children, either their whole bodies cut out of a photograph or just their faces. They can role-play through the stories, which encourages their social and emotional development. Continue to add to this felt collection over time.

Multisensory Explorations

Add textured embellishments to the pieces, such as gluing sand to a piece to represent the beach or attaching foil to make a mirror. Glue buttons or sequins or other craft items on the board to enrich the senses.

Diversity Adaptations

Include pictures of real people of diverse cultures doing nonstereotypical activities (Asian woman as a construction foreperson, Latino man as a judge, elderly woman as a fitness instructor). Use felt or cloth in an array of colors beyond the primary variety and be sure to include earth tones and pastels, allowing children to use colors of the earth.

Fingerplays

Intended Ages
infancy and older

Brain Connections
receptive and expressive language, listening

Materials Needed
none

Try fingerplays such as this one to engage children in expressive and receptive language combined with sensorimotor activity. This fingerplay is about the hands and fingers. Using tried-and-true fingerplays and rhymes continues the tradition of passing along culture to future generations. By combining words and actions, you are creating additional pathways in the brain.

Open, Shut Them

Open, shut them, open, shut them,
Give a little clap.
Open, shut them, open, shut them,
Put them in your lap.

Creep them, creep them, creep them,
    creep them
Right up to your chin.
Open wide your smiling mouth,
But do not let them in.

Creep them, creep them, creep them,
    creep them
Right down to your toes.
Let them fly up in the air and
Bop you in the nose!

Open, shut them, open, shut them,
Give a little clap.

Open, shut them, open, shut them,
Put them in your lap.

Extension Activities
Enhance vocabulary by using the word *phalanges* for fingers. Learn this fingerplay in sign language or add music and sing it!

Multisensory Explorations
Wear gloves when doing this fingerplay.

Diversity Adaptations
Learn stories, songs, and rhymes from other cultures to share as fingerplays. When I took my children to Africa to visit their great-grandfather, he told them a story (I later learned was an African folktale) about a mosquito that whispers into the ear of a hunter and tricks him not to hunt his friends in the savannah. I could never find the origin of that folktale, but I came home and tried to create my own fingerplay to tell the tale.

> "Whisper, whisper, Mr. Mosquito, into the hunter's ear." (Children rub two fingers against their thumb and hold it over their ear.)

> "Be a good gentleman and run away; my friends and I want to play today!"

I'd then have the children use their "mosquitoes" to whisper into their friends' ears what they wanted to play that day. The children would then talk about what some of the suggestions for play were. It was a good circle time transition to playtime (or center time).
    Be creative!

Deciphering Decibels

Intended Ages

two years and older

Brain Connections

auditory processing, expressive and receptive language, listening, predicting

Materials Needed

- objects that emit sounds (ticking clock, blowing fan, radio)

Being able to discriminate between different sounds is a vital role in understanding spoken language. Use this activity to help children isolate specific sounds from the normal sounds of the day.

Hide objects that make sounds around the room. Have children listen for them, describe what they hear, and predict what is making the noise. Being able to decipher sounds will help children learn to hear the sounds that words make.

Extension Activities

Go for a walk outside, and listen to the sounds (cars passing, birds singing, wind blowing, dogs barking). Record on a chart the kinds of sounds you hear. Do you hear the same sounds at different times of day? Or are there morning sounds, afternoon sounds, and nighttime sounds?

Multisensory Explorations

Gather materials that make different sounds (dry leaves, rice shakers, marbles in a glass jar, nuts and bolts, cellophane, and other noisy stuff), and have children guess what is making the sound.

Diversity Adaptations

Play sounds of instruments from different cultures for the children (steel drum, bagpipe, kalimba, sitar, etc.).

MATHEMATICS

Brain Connections

Mathematical thinking skills build strong brain connections through music, organization, seriation, spatial awareness, predicting, and problem solving. For example, learning how to play a musical instrument or how to read music or sing a song, strengthens the corpus callosum, which connects both hemispheres of the brain.

While such connections and complexity are the root of creativity, math should be kept simple. Try taking this quiz, and see how you do with keeping it simple.

1. How do you put an elephant into the refrigerator?

Think you know? Here's the answer: *Open the door, put in the elephant, and close the door.*

2. How do you put a giraffe into the refrigerator?

This is a bit trickier. Are you ready? *Open the door, take out the elephant, and put in the giraffe.*

3. The lion is having a party, and all of the animals show up except one. Who's missing?

Think you got it? Need more time? *It's the giraffe. He's still in the refrigerator.*

How well did you do? Did you get three out of three? When it comes to math, young children need good investigative skills to be good problem solvers. Sometimes keeping it simple is harder than it looks. Work with small bits of information until children are comfortable with the idea. My dear friend Dawn Jones, a first-grade teacher, says she likes to think of this as dropping bread crumbs. Each new idea is a bread crumb. She drops little clues about where she's going, but she doesn't move on until she can tell the children have started to pick them up and follow along. If the children are stuck and can't figure out how to pick up the pieces, she starts over with a new approach.

Children gain number sense when they have early and repeated opportunities to think about numbers in relation to something tangible. When children learn how to divide something equally, to make predictions, and to play games that require matching, counting, adding, and subtracting, they are developing their number sense. Without a connection to prior knowledge, children are more likely to have difficulties when adults assume they can just "teach" a child math. Multiple inputs from various mathematical concepts are necessary to help children have a good sense of numbers and ultimately strong math skills.

The most effective early math experiences need to be hands-on and filled with play and exploration. Gaining math skills allows children to explore such concepts as structure, space, quantity, change, time, and music. The brain-based math activities that follow are sure to give little problem solvers plenty of chances to grow their brains!

Supporting Math in the Environment

Math is used every day. While math opportunities can be found everywhere, it helps to stock your environment with materials that you know play an intentional role in developing math and numeracy skills. The more creative, the better. If you can imagine it, do it!

For example, you can support math in the environment by counting manipulatives of various sizes and in large quantities. The manipulatives can be recycled items, such as bottle caps, baby food lids, jars, etc. You can also use store-bought articles, such as bugs, teddy bears, or other items purchased from school supply companies. Buy items from a home improvement store, such as pieces of pipe (plastic or metal with no sharp edges), bolts, nuts, and large screws. As with all manipulatives, always be sure the items are large enough not to cause a choking hazard and do not have sharp edges that could cut a child.

Here are some other items to use in facilitating the development of math skills:

- measuring scale
- balance scale
- rulers
- containers for water and dry material
- paper

- pencils/crayons/chalk/paint
- blocks
- sand
- water
- weights

Mathematics and Infants

You may believe that infants aren't capable of understanding mathematical concepts at such a young age. That may be true of algebra (heck, I still don't get it), but it is not true of the simple concept of adding and taking away. Although infants lack language skills, they can still process receptive language about math concepts. They listen to your words and look to you for clues. They use visual and auditory discrimination to look for connections. They use all their senses to take in the world around them and to make meaning. A game such as peekaboo is early math. "Where's Taylor?" "There she is!" First something wasn't there, and then it was. Nothing plus Taylor is one Taylor.

Through everyday contact with infants, you can continually reinforce math skills. Diaper changing is a wonderful learning time. Here you have close proximity to the infant, and you have his undivided attention. Lift one leg at a time while saying, "Hayden has one leg. Hayden has two legs." Repeat the process with all the body parts. "Hayden has one nose. Hayden has two eyes. Hayden has four teeth." You'll soon discover that math for infants can be found everywhere.

Selecting Books to Support Math

Build a math vocabulary by teaching children how to use such words as *longer, shorter, bigger, smaller, more, less, up, down, square, round, rectangular, hard, crunchy, soft, mushy, empty, full, equal,* and so on. Lots of books have math concepts embedded in them, especially books with patterns or predictability. And when reading any book, point out numbers and shapes in the illustrations. For instance, in a book about pumpkins, point out the shapes of the eyes. "What shape are the pumpkin's eyes?" Shapes are math!

SUGGESTED BOOKS—AGES BIRTH TO FOUR

Fromental, Jean-Luc, and Joëlle Jolivet. 2006. *365 penguins.* New York: Abrams Books for Young Readers.

Martin, Bill, Jr. 1989. *Chicka chicka boom boom*. Illustrated by Lois Ehlert. New York: Simon & Schuster.

Seuss, Dr. 1960. *One fish, two fish, red fish, blue fish*. New York: Random House.

————. 1989. *Ten apples up on top*. New York: Random House.

SUGGESTED BOOKS—AGES FIVE TO EIGHT

Anno, Masaichiro, and Mitsumasa Anno. 1983. *Anno's mysterious multiplying jar*. New York: Philomel Books.

Leedy, Loreen. 1997. *Mission: Addition*. New York: Holiday House.

Murphy, Stuart J. 2004. *Tally O'Malley*. Illustrated by Cynthia Jabar. New York: HarperCollins.

Seeger, Laura Vaccaro. 2008. *One boy*. New York: Roaring Brook Press.

Pitter-Pat Patterns

Intended Ages

eighteen months and older

Brain Connections

gross-motor skills, sequencing, patterning, contrast

Materials Needed

- music

Ah, who doesn't love the pitter-patter of tiny feet? Set those patters to music and motion, and you can have quite a party! Get those feet on the floor to dance, dance, and dance some more!

Use your body to move in patterns. Do a motion, and have the children copy you. Skip, hop, jump. Skip, hop, jump. Skip, skip, hop, hop, jump, jump. Have the children take turns creating the pattern the group will follow. Add music for more creative mathematical fun!

Dancing as a pair is a way to introduce the concept of one-to-one ratio. By holding hands with a toddler, you can take a step and wait for her to take a step to follow you. Take slow and deliberate steps, allowing time for the child to follow. Be sure to count the steps out loud as you move to the music.

Extension Activities

Put words on the ground or use tape to make prompts reinforcing the patterns.

Multisensory Explorations

Play music, and have a person call out the pattern so children have to listen for the cues.

Diversity Adaptations

Learning how to move in rhythmic ways like a belly dancer or an Irish step dancer or an Appalachian clogger is a great way to learn about different cultures! Invite in "guest instructors" to teach children some of these dance moves. Be careful not to play music from a different culture and assume that any movement is an authentic form of dance. Take the time to learn about the way the dance is performed and then practice those movements to the music. Be sure to include music from various parts of the country, such as country music, New Orleans jazz, and African drums. We have a lot of diversity right here in the United States.

Ten in the Bed Counting Sticks

Intended Ages

four years and older

Brain Connections

counting, classifying, receptive and expressive language

Materials Needed

- ten craft sticks, numbered 1–10 (written as one, two, three and/or 1, 2, 3)
- construction paper
- the children's book *Ten in the Bed* by Jane Cabrera (Holiday House 2010)
- glue

"There were ten in the bed, and the little one said, 'Roll over, roll over.'" Have you heard this counting rhyme before? It's been made into a great math book incorporating song and rhythm, and the story is probably familiar to anyone who ever had to share a bed with a child. There is never enough room, especially if the little one sleeps like a starfish.

Sing the verses to the story as you read *Ten in the Bed.* Then have the children construct a pocket bed out of two pieces of construction paper glued on three sides that is big enough to hold ten craft sticks. Children can practice counting the sticks as they place them in the bed, lining up the sticks in numerical order.

Extension Activities

Create a chart counting the number of dads, moms, sisters, brothers, grandparents, and even pets such as dogs and cats in the children's families. This helps children begin to visualize quantity.

Talk about family compositions and vocabulary: Do you have one dad? Do you have one mom? Do you have one sister? Do you have one brother?

Discuss the many words used to describe family members, such as Grandpa, Pop Pop, Gramps, Pappy, Poppy, Abuelo; Grandma, Memaw, Grammy, Grams, Nanna, Abuela.

Multisensory Explorations

Use emery boards instead of popsicle sticks; they have a rough surface like sandpaper.

Diversity Adaptations

Create Spanish (or other language) counting sticks. Tell the story using a different word for bed that might be found in a different culture; for example, "Ten in the hammock, and the little one said, 'Roll over. . . .'"

Keep in mind as you discuss family composition with children that you need to be inclusive of all types of families, including single-parent, adoptive parent, same-sex parent, and families headed by grandparent(s).

Patchwork Patterns

Intended Ages

three years and older

Brain Connections

visual discrimination, matching, patterning

Materials Needed

- fabric or other materials to create textured swatches

Quilts and patchwork have a long tradition in many cultures. Besides being a way to tell a story through shapes and colors, quilts also reinforce math concepts, such as symmetry and fractions. Children can use patchwork patterns to tell their own stories and build social and emotional skills while strengthening their math skills.

Give each child a swatch, and have the children as a group make a pattern by standing in a line or other formation. Have them look for patterns they make when they hold up their different swatches. Children can make as many patterns as they want with all different kinds of textures and colors.

Extension Activities

Children can combine swatches and create a classroom quilt. Over time they can continue to add to the quilt and/or add words to their swatches. Words could be children's names or positive attributes of each child or other words to build social-emotional connections.

Multisensory Explorations

Include different sizes of swatches and a variety of textures.

Diversity Adaptations

Use fabric or materials to create the textures or patterns on the swatches that represent diverse cultures. Batik patterns that use removable wax to cover the parts of the fabric that won't be dyed have been traced to Asia and India. Kente cloth is a traditional African pattern of woven silks and cottons. Damask is a weave of cotton and twill found in Middle Eastern countries. Invite children to make use of these patterns to create colorful quilts.

One of These Things Is Not Like the Others

Intended Ages
two years and older

Brain Connections
convergent thinking, comparing, deducing

Materials Needed
- sets of like objects (cars, shapes, food, animals, blocks) with multiple objects having similar characteristics

I will always remember the segment on *Sesame Street* when the voice would sing, "One of these things is not like the others." The screen would flash four objects, but only three would have something in common. The viewers' job was to figure out which item didn't fit. This is the same game, although the children get to group the items from an assortment of objects, and they can regroup the items based on similar characteristics.

Give children sets of objects and have them sort the objects by characteristics. One method might be to put all the cars together as a group, all the shapes together as a group, and so on. Then have the children group the objects by a different characteristic, such as color. For example, the banana, the bus, and the chicken are all yellow. Ask children to share with the group how each item in the group fits the characteristic.

Extension Activities
Even within the groups the children could regroup. For example, they could sort all the cars into subgroups: cars with two doors and cars with four doors.

Multisensory Explorations
Include items with varied characteristics, such as smooth, rough, dull, shiny, scented, etc.

Diversity Adaptations
Use items that might be found in a variety of cultures but have the same use. For example, for the category of eating utensils, have children sort spoons and forks made from plastic, metal, and wood; chopsticks; sporks; etc. For the category of transportation, items could include horse and cart, bicycle, and wagon, along with cars and trucks.

Budding Builders

Intended Ages
one year and older

Brain Connections
observing, predicting, cause and effect, sensorimotor skills

Materials Needed
- wooden blocks of various sizes, shapes, and weights

Block play is vital in helping children understand shapes and spatial relationships. Blocks can be used to build structures, can be ordered by size or shape, and can be used to explore mathematical concepts like leverage, slopes, and inclines.

Create an inviting space for children to experience block play. Play should be child-centered, although you can control which blocks you make available at what times. You can put specific blocks out, like wedges to create slopes and inclines, and include balls, cars, or anything else with wheels to demonstrate velocity and acceleration.

Extension Activities
Add manipulatives to change the nature of the play. Add realistic people figures, house objects, profession-related objects, books, and art tools. Children can create sculptures and then draw them on paper.

Multisensory Explorations
Include blocks or manipulatives that have different textures, weights, and colors. Cover some blocks with felt or sandpaper.

Diversity Adaptations
Include shapes and types of materials that could represent architecture in other countries. Straw could be introduced as a material for a roof, and dowels could be used to make pylons. Bring in picture books that show architecture in different countries and that illustrate what life might be like in a house sitting on the top of the Himalayas. Use photos of people (including people of color and people with disabilities) to tape onto blocks to use as props in block play.

Everyday Math

Intended Ages
three years and older

Brain Connections
patterning, classifying, creative thinking

Materials Needed
- tableware
- food items

Who knew mealtime was really a mathematical smorgasbord? With all that patterning and classifying, it's no wonder we work up an appetite.

Meals are a great way to practice math skills. Have the children count the number of plates they need for all children present. Use a one-to-one ratio to add a fork beside each plate. Make a pattern with tableware—plate, fork, cup, plate, fork, cup—as you go around the table. Children can count out food items as they are distributed. "Three chicken nuggets, two apple slices."

Extension Activities
Although we tend to think of everyday math as being the most obvious at mealtime, look for it elsewhere. You might be surprised. "How many steps does it take to get to the bathroom to wash our hands?" "How high is the light switch?" "How many beats are in this song?"

Multisensory Explorations
Have children touch each item as it's counted.

Diversity Adaptations
Count in a language other than English.

Big Shoes to Fill

Intended Ages
three years and older

Brain Connections
classifying, patterning motor skills, spatial awareness, and expressive language

Materials Needed
- spare (not children's daily wear shoes)* shoes with clearly patterned tread
- water-based paint
- brushes (if necessary)
- sheets of paper or foam

*Ask for donated shoes from families or buy used shoes from discount or secondhand stores so that children won't damage their daily wear shoes.

I remember being embarrassed when I was in the third grade and my mother bought me a pair of shoes that had Big Bird on the left sole and Cookie Monster on the right sole. That happened to be the first year I played softball, and you could see alternating tracks of Big Bird and Cookie Monster going around the bases. Although I didn't appreciate it at the time, those shoes were brain-based. I was able to build motor skills, patterning, spatial awareness, and expressive language all while leaving imprints in the dirt. Who knew?

Make prints of shoe treads on pieces of paper. Ask children questions to describe the tread: "Are the shapes similar or different?" "Are the shoe sizes similar or different?" "Do big shoes have the same kinds of shapes as each other? Do small shoes?" Ask children to share some of their observations.

Extension Activities
Depending on the design of the sole imprint, you could even take the dried picture and use a pencil to trace a way out of the maze. Make an imprint on a piece of foam and leave a trail. Have children "track" a tread to find out what made the shape.

Multisensory Explorations
Use sand in the paint when creating the imprint, or use different types of paper.

Diversity Adaptations
Include shoes found in a variety of cultures. Ask parents to bring in shoes that could tolerate washable paint.

fraction food

Intended Ages

four years and older

Brain Connections

Problem solving, comparing, estimating

Materials Needed

- paper plates or construction paper circles
- triangle shapes cut from construction paper

  or

- pizza dough rounds
- toppings

What's not to love about pizza as a math tool? It's round (that's a shape). It can be divided into more pieces (fractions to demonstrate parts of the whole). It can have other objects added to it (cheese, pepperoni, mushrooms, olives), and you can subtract the fraction when you eat it!

Use paper plates or construction paper to create circles like the shape of a pizza. Cut triangles out of construction paper to make pizza slices. Experiment with different widths of slices to see how many fraction possibilities you can make.

Once you have the pizza slices you can create different types of "toppings" on the pizza to extend the math activity. Children can use con-struction paper to cut different shapes and colors of pretend food, like "round" pepperoni, "black" olives, "white" onions, etc., and then practice counting the items as they place them on the pizza slices. These items can be glued to create a permanent reminder of the activity, or the items can be left unglued and recycled for the next activity.

Extension Activities

Teach sharing by cutting something desirable into pieces. When one child cuts the cookie and the other child chooses which part she wants, children learn the value of being fair.

Multisensory Explorations

Make pizzas with dough, sauce, and toppings. Once prepared, the pizzas can be cut into different shapes.

When using foods children will be eating, be mindful of any food allergies. For example, if you have a child on a gluten-free diet, be sure not to use wheat-based dough.

Diversity Adaptations

Use different types of toppings for the pizza that might be a staple in different cultures, as well as different crusts for the pizza, such as pita, matzo, parantha, poori, chapati, or tortillas.

Subatize!

Intended Ages

six years and older

Brain Connections

whole/part thinking, problem solving, classifying, flexible thinking

Materials Needed

- blank index cards
- sticker dots or marker to make dots

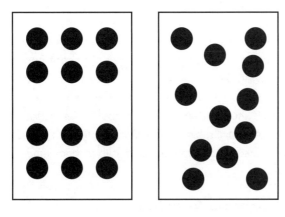

I love this idea! *Subatize*, pronounced "soo-buh-tize," means to see things as a group. The skill is critical for making mathematical estimations. Simply put, if you can subatize, you can recognize a group and just "know" it's a group without counting. It's this perceptual skill that contributes to children's ability to understand parts and wholes.

Use index cards to create subatizing flash cards. You will make two sets of cards. The first card will have the number of dots placed in dice formation on the card. The second card will have the same number, but the dots will be in a random formation.

Quickly flash the card with the random pattern in front of the child, and see if she can tell you how many dots there are. Then, without confirming her guess, flash the second card with dots in dice formation, and ask if she can guess how many there are this time. Chances are good she will guess the answer more accurately for the second card.

Extension Activities

Cards can be created with different shapes besides dots. Group objects by type, such as cars or animals. Use the same shape formation on the cards as you did with the dots.

Multisensory Explorations

Use different colored stickers or dots to create the subatizing cards. Cards can be created with different textures, such as sandpaper or high-gloss paper.

Diversity Adaptations

To diversify your game, you could use hieroglyphics, Chinese, or Greek characters. Please make sure you know what the symbols mean if you chose to use these on the cards.

Petals around the Rose

Intended Ages

seven years and older

Brain Connections

deductive reasoning, flexible thinking, problem solving

Materials Needed

- six dice

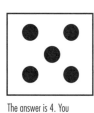

The answer is 2. You only count the petals, not the rose.

The answer is 4. You only count the petals, not the rose.

The answer is 0. There are petals but no rose.

The answer is 0. There is a rose but no petals.

This is a cool game—although it's not one that a child will enjoy playing over and over. But it's exciting the first time they get it!

Have children gather around you in a circle so they can see you shake the dice and roll all six dice onto a flat surface.

While you are shaking the dice, tell the children, "The name of the game is 'Petals around the Rose.' The name is important. The answer is always an even number."

Roll the dice, and wait a few seconds for the children to try and guess the answer. Tell the children what the answer is depending on the roll. You only count the dice that have both a rose and petals. The dot in the middle is the rose, and the dots around the center (the rose) are the petals. So you only ever count the three or the five on the dice. If it's a three, you count two petals. If it's a five, you count four petals. When you add up any combination of these dice, you will get an even number. You don't count the center dot (the rose); you only count the outside dots (the petals).

Repeat the phrase, the rolling of the dice, and the counting of the petals as many times as necessary, until the children begin to consistently get the same answer. Children will want you to answer their inquiries in between rolls. Don't answer. Just keep rolling until they begin to show signs they understand. This could take a dozen or more rolls. Seriously! Do it as many times as necessary. Be patient, and allow them time to think.

Extension Activities

Don't teach all of the children at once. Have one child teach another child, and so on, until everyone gets it.

Multisensory Explorations

Allow children to hold, shake, and roll the dice.

Diversity Adaptations

Vary the length of time you repeat each roll to allow children more time if necessary. Some children will need more time than others.

SCIENCE

Brain Connections

When it comes to science, both hemispheres play a vital role. The left brain processes observations, predictions, experiments, and evaluations. The right brain controls curiosity. Without curiosity you wouldn't take your exploration very far.

Children are born curious. They are natural scientists. And with our help, they remain curious for the better part of their lives.

In general, three types of scientific inquiry occur in an early education environment. The first is formal science, in which the teacher plans an activity to teach a specific skill. The second type is informal science, which requires little or no teacher involvement. Children work at their own pace, giving the activity as much or as little attention as they like. And finally there is incidental science, which falls into the area teachers like to call "teachable moments." These are the events we cannot plan or initiate without the help of nature or the convergence of events beyond our control. Think of coming upon a beautiful spiderweb spun in an unusual place. How wonderful is it to see a double rainbow (or even a single rainbow, for that matter) or the roots of a massive tree that was blown over in a storm? We don't plan for these things to happen, but we want to help children experience them fully when they do.

Although the activities in this book are distinctly of the first variety, always allow children to discover opportunities on their own. Allow some children more time with the materials if they want, even after other children have moved on. Even the most skilled educators have no way of knowing when a child has had his fill of discovery. A child's wonder is like a circle with no end.

Supporting Science in the Environment

Science is everywhere if you know how to look for it. In fact, observation is a basic skill of science. In order to be investigators, it helps to have a variety of tools available. The following materials (combined with your good ideas) are a great way to start your scientists on their way to a world of discovery:

- magnifying glasses
- test tubes
- funnels
- living organisms
- weights
- scales
- pulleys
- ramps
- microscopes
- tweezers
- rubber bands
- things with wheels
- things that fly
- things that stink
- things that are gooey

You get the idea!

Science and Infants

Infants are born scientists. They have an incredible ability to use their senses to take in the world around them. They are deft observers, and no keener brain function is at work during infancy than when the mirror neuron is firing. When infants watch what another person is doing, their mirror neuron begins to fire, causing them to repeat the behavior they just watched. Smile at a baby and watch her smile back. Make a funny face and watch her try to make the same face. Sometimes infants lack the motor control to duplicate the face, but they will be doing their best to mirror what they see and hear.

Scientific exploration abounds when infants are given a variety of objects that they can use all of their senses to investigate. Whether homemade or store bought, "toys" (meaning anything you give a child to play with) should be intentionally selected to be safe and stimulating. Clear plastic bottles with different colors of water are fun to roll on the ground, shake, feel the weight of in their hands, and look through to see the colors. Give infants a chance to explore real objects such as cooking utensils, dishes, pots and pans, and items found in the natural environment, such as dirt (they usually find that on their own), clay, grass, sand, and water. Let them fully explore the world around them, providing you have made it safe (removed small objects that could be choking hazards). But remember to be there to ask questions ("Did you see that butterfly?") to use receptive language and to help guide their discovery.

Selecting Books and Resources for Science

My favorite science dude is Steve Spangler. Visit his Web site at www .stevespangler.com for good ideas. You can buy the materials for his projects there, or you can make many of the items yourself. Try to recycle as many items as you can.

A good place to start when selecting science books is choosing books about the topics the children are interested in. Ask the children questions about the kinds of things they want to learn about. When you have a good idea of their interests, head out to the public library, and find books with age-appropriate language and illustrations. Choose a variety of books on the same topic, and provide children a wide range of opportunities to explore the subject.

SUGGESTED BOOKS—AGES BIRTH TO FOUR

Allen, Pamela. 1996. *Who sank the boat?* New York: Putnam Juvenile.

Kudlinski, Kathleen V. 2008. *Boy, were we wrong about dinosaurs!* Illustrated by S. D. Shindler. New York: Puffin Books.

Oliver, Narelle. 1997. *The hunt.* Melbourne, Australia: Lothian Books.

Pallotta, Jerry. 1989. *The ocean alphabet book.* Illustrated by Frank Mazzola Jr. Watertown, MA: Charlesbridge Publishing.

SUGGESTED BOOKS—AGES FIVE TO EIGHT

Fleming, Denise. 2007. *In the small, small pond.* New York: Henry Holt and Co. BYR Paperbacks.

Metzger, Steve. 2007. *The leaves are falling one by one.* New York: Scholastic.

Musgrove, Margaret. 2001. *The spider weaver: A legend of kente cloth.* Illustrated by Julia Cairns. New York: Blue Sky Press.

Ripley, Catherine. 2004. *Why? The best ever question and answer book about nature, science, and the world around you.* Illustrated by Scot Ritchie. Toronto, Ontario: Maple Tree Press.

Tubular Flatulence

Intended Ages
five years and older

Brain Connections
cause and effect, observing, predicting

Materials Needed
- *The Gas We Pass: The Story of Farts* by Shinta Cho (Kane/Miller 2001)
- "test tubes"*
- water
- vegetable oil
- Alka-Seltzer tablets or Tub Tints (effervescent color tablets)

*For the test tubes, two-liter bottles that haven't been expanded yet work great! They look like beakers but are indestructible and fun to explain. You can buy these through school supply companies. Or you can use eight-ounce water bottles instead.

The brain loves it when real life combines with abstract thought. When children make connections between something their own bodies do naturally and spontaneously and something they read about bodies doing in a book, their knowledge about their bodies is reinforced. This type of connection is called text-to-self connection, and making text-to-self connections helps them picture how they fit into the world around them. For young children, ideas presented in books often seem abstract. If they can see how something they do is presented in a book, they begin to realize that books aren't always about abstract things—that the words on the pages can have meaning in real life.

This is a fun activity to demonstrate how our bodies break down and release gas. Even very young children know what a toot is, even if they don't know what creates it. As an adult, you might be thinking this is a silly, or even offensive, activity, and you may not be comfortable with it. But children love to talk about their bodies and the magic they can produce with it. You will have a rapt audience with this activity.

Begin by reading the book *The Gas We Pass* to the children. Ask them what they know about how the gas comes out and how it got there in the first place. Then demonstrate how our bodies are like a bottle: Fill a bottle three-quarters full with oil. Then fill the remaining space with water. Add the Alka-Seltzer or Tub Tints tablet to the bottle, and explain how the tablet doesn't begin to dissolve or change color until it reaches the water. Without capping the bottle, watch as the tablet dissolves and the gas bubbles rise to the top of the bottle and pop. Once the gas is released, the bubbles slowly begin to fall to the bottom of the bottle. Then the bubbles pop, releasing the gas.

Extension Activities
This same activity can be done to create different kinds of bottles, such as lava lamps or "ocean in a bottle." These kinds of bottles can demonstrate how elements, such as oil and water, work together. You can also include items such as sand, small toys, and so forth, to create a soothing scene.

Multisensory Explorations
Use scented oil to create a different sensory experience.

Diversity Adaptations

Some cultures and families are not comfortable discussing bodily functions. Be respectful of this perspective, and adapt your language accordingly. While you're on the subject of oil, many cultures use different kinds of oils for cooking and also for lamps. Stories such as the Arabic folktale "Aladdin and the Magic Lamp" or the origin of the Jewish holiday of Hanukkah, the celebration of lights, can help you teach about how important oil is around the globe.

What Happens If...?

Intended Ages
four years and older

Brain Connections
cause and effect, predicting, problem solving, expressive and receptive language

Materials Needed
- balls
- blocks
- water
- paper
- rubber bands
- wedge blocks (inclines)

If I poke my sister in the eye, she'll probably throw something at me. This example demonstrates cause and effect—but not in the most constructive way. Let's try something else. If I build a tower and place the largest object on the top, it will fall over. If I put water on paper, it will change its composition, and my paper won't be good to write on anymore. But if I let it dry out, then I can write on it again.

By helping children make predictions, we are helping them make connections between their prior learning and their future learning. Use the materials to model how cause and effect works in order to practice making predictions: "Hey, I have a ramp, and I have a ball. What do you think would happen if I let go of the ball at the top of the ramp?" "What do you think would happen if I let go of the ball at the bottom of the ramp?" "What do you think would happen if I put the ramp on the ball?" "What do you think would happen if I put the ball on my head?"

Choose from the items in the materials list (or add more), and allow children to create their own cause-and-effect scenarios. Be sure to engage children in the process of predicting what is going to happen and discussing whether the prediction was accurate.

Extension Activities
Help children verbalize their thought process by developing cause-and-effect questioning to use in everyday work. Ask children questions like "What would happen if we walked backward to the playground?" They go there every day, and they've probably never thought about what would happen if something changed their routine. Take this opportunity to make plans based on the results of the predictions. Make a chart or other visual diagrams to illustrate the possibilities.

Multisensory Explorations
Provide open-ended activities with multisensory opportunities. Be as creative (and messy) as you can stand by allowing children to make predictions with unpredictable materials. Gooey things are unpredictable. Will it flop out of the bowl? Will it stick to the carpet? Will it hold a shape for more than a minute? The more multisensory the materials, the more you can expand on the predictions of cause and effect. The possibilities are endless.

Diversity Adaptations

For some children, effects of certain causes (behavior, for example) may not receive the same response in one culture as they do in another. Allow children to express what they believe are the effects of the causes as they relate to their prior knowledge.

Sensory Exchange

Intended Ages

three years and older

Brain Connections

flexible thinking, perceptual-motor skills, creative thinking

Materials Needed

- gloves (nonlatex, winter)
- paper
- pencils
- blindfold
- puzzle or blocks

Ever wondered if it's true about other senses taking over if one becomes impaired? Try it out. If you can't see, can your hands be your eyes for you? If you don't have the full sensory effect in your fingers, can you still complete a puzzle? Let's give it a try.

What happens if you change how you use your senses? Have the children put on gloves to do a puzzle or build with blocks; have them use their feet to draw a picture. Blindfold the children, and have them complete a puzzle without looking. When everyone has had an opportunity to work with gloves and blindfolds, have children share their perceptions of how the activity was the same as and different from doing it regularly.

Extension Activities

Have the children try to complete an obstacle course while blindfolded.

Multisensory Explorations

Use gloves with bumps on them, or have the children use only one hand. Release scents into the air while they attempt to do the obstacle course.

Diversity Adaptations

Use scents from different cultures or tactile games that include different visual cues.

Bottled Up from the Bottom Up

Intended Ages

four years and older

Brain Connections

observing, patterning

Materials Needed

- mason jars or baby food jars
- sand
- topsoil
- rocks

It's difficult for children to understand that there are layers to the earth. When you bottle layers of sediment, though, children can see how the earth is composed.

Give each child a jar, and explain how the earth has many layers. Have children start with rocks, then add a layer of sand and a layer of topsoil. When the children are finished, talk about how they have made a miniature model of what the earth looks like inside.

Extension Activities

Use colorful sand to create a sandscape in a bottle, not only to demonstrate the earth's layers, but to use as a centerpiece or paperweight.

Multisensory Explorations

Add other items to the jar, such as shells or smaller pebbles, or plant a seed.

Diversity Adaptations

Use different colored sand and types of dirt that might be found in different places in the world.

Delicious DNA

Intended Ages

six years and older

Brain Connections

perceptual-motor skills, critical thinking

Materials Needed

- blunt-edged toothpicks
- mini marshmallows (four or more colors)
- licorice strands
- paper
- markers
- book(s) by Frances R. Balkwill and Mic Rolph

Now here's some science you can sink your teeth into. Helping children understand something as complex as DNA can be fun and easy with marshmallows and licorice to demonstrate how the molecules cling together to form a double helix. Using a pincer grip to place the marshmallow on a blunt-edged toothpick builds fine-motor skills. This activity also develops critical-thinking skills.

Gather the children around you, and ask them if they know how they got their color of hair, eyes, or skin or how tall they are going to be. Each child can create a chart of his or her characteristics (blue eyes, red hair, three feet tall, freckles, shoe size 3—the more, the better). Then to help explain where the characteristics come from and what cells and DNA are, I suggest books by Frances R. Balkwill and Mic Rolph. This duo has written a series of books explaining DNA and cells for children:

Enjoy Your Cells
Have a Nice DNA
DNA Is Here to Stay
Amazing Schemes within Your Genes
Cells Are Us

To further illustrate what DNA looks like, go back to the characteristics chart and ask children to choose different colored marshmallows to represent each characteristic. Once they have mapped out the marshmallows to go with the characteristics, demonstrate how to stick the marshmallows onto the toothpicks. Then connect the toothpicks to licorice strands on each end, starting at the bottom and working up to create a ladder. Space the toothpicks about an inch apart. After the two pieces of licorice are connected by the toothpicks, twist the ladder to represent the double helix.

Explain that each ladder represents the parts that make each person unique. Have children show each other their double helix to show how everyone's is different, even for members of the same family. Children can decide if they want to display their double helix or have it for a snack. Either way it's fun!

Extension Activities

Construct larger models more accurately with gummy bears connecting to the marshmallows to show how the molecules are literally attached. Use two different colors of licorice as well.

Multisensory Explorations

Use scented marshmallows or flavored toothpicks.

Diversity Adaptations

Instead of marshmallows, use foods like pasta or rice, which can be glued on paper with yarn instead of licorice.

Evaporation Exploration

Intended Ages

four years and older

Brain Connections

predicting, problem solving, observing

Materials Needed

- blackboard
- sponge
- water

We know rain falls down, but where does water go when it's on the ground? Try this activity to help children understand how water evaporates.

Wet a sponge, and make a broad stroke across the blackboard. Have the children observe what happens for several minutes. Discuss what the children have observed, and ask what happened. End the discussion by explaining that water evaporates: it turns from liquid into a gas and becomes part of the air.

Extension Activities

Repeat this activity, but instead of making one streak, make two about a yard apart. Use a piece of cardboard to fan one of the streaks. Ask children to predict which one will disappear faster and why.

Multisensory Explorations

Wet different surfaces (bumpy blacktop, smooth chalkboard, rough wooden bench) to see if the water evaporates the same way.

Diversity Adaptations

Explain to the children that in some places on earth there is very little water—in deserts, for example. Talk about how people are careful in these places to keep water from evaporating. They conserve their use of water so that they will have enough. After experimenting with different techniques, see if you can discover which method caused the water to evaporate slowest. Use this technique to demonstrate conservation.

You Are What You Eat

Intended Ages

four years and older

Brain Connections

predicting, observing, problem solving

Materials Needed

- one cup of original Total cereal
- one-quarter cup of water
- sandwich-size resealable bag
- large magnet

Have you ever tried to explain to children about the value of minerals in our food? Have you tried to explain that iron is actually in food? Try this experiment to help them see it for themselves.

Place a cup of Total cereal inside a resealable baggie. (I use Total because it has a high iron content and the flakes break down without any hard chunks.) Then pour a quarter cup of water into the bag and seal it. Squish and mash until the flakes are practically liquid. Next, take a magnet, and rest it in your palm, placing the bag of mushy flakes on top of the magnet. Swish your hand in a circular motion for about fifteen seconds, and then quickly flip the bag over and use the magnet to pull the iron across the surface of the bag.

After the bag has rested on top of your hand, the iron will sink to the bottom of the bag and be attracted to the magnet, even though the plastic separates the two. When you flip the bag over, the iron is still attracted to the magnet, and if you drag the magnet across the bag, the iron particles will follow the magnet so that the children can see the iron.

Extension Activities

Experiment with different kinds of cereal to see if you get the same reaction. Look for other food items that contain high amounts of iron that you could experiment with.

Multisensory Explorations

Use hands to squish the cereal with water, or place the magnet directly in the mixture.

Diversity Adaptations

Have the children learn about the types of food people in various cultures eat and if the foods have the same vitamins and minerals in them as the food they eat. Gather product labels from different foods to compare with the foods the children typically eat.

Rotation Relation

Intended Ages
three years and older

Brain Connections
predicting, problem solving

Materials Needed
- flat outdoor surface area or large sheets of paper
- chalk

"Me and my shadow, strolling down the avenue." What makes that shadow anyway? Does the shadow change depending on the weather? Time of day?

Pick a sunny day, and go outside. Have children take turns tracing each other's shadows with chalk. A hard surface, such as a patio, driveway, or blacktop works best, but you can also use a large sheet of paper as long as you don't move its position.

Start in the morning, and have each child face in the same direction. Her partner (or you) will trace the outline her shadow makes on the ground. At noon repeat this process, and compare how the shadow has changed. At late afternoon repeat this process again. Now that you have three shapes to compare, discuss why the shadow keeps moving even though the children never moved. How much did the shadow move? Did the shape of the shadow change? How? Why?

Extension Activities
Chart other things in the environment to see if their shadows are affected by the rotation of the earth.

Multisensory Explorations
Use different surfaces to see if the shadow is affected by the change. Instead of drawing on paper, draw directly on the blacktop. Does the bumpy surface of the blacktop affect the shadow?

Diversity Adaptations
Different geographical locations have different amounts of alternating sun and clouds. In the Pacific Northwest of the United States, rain clouds keep the sun from shining a good bit of the time. It might be unpredictable to plan this type of activity there because you may not have the sun available when you want to do it. You could turn the activity into a weather lesson and use predictions to plan for a sunny day when this activity would work.

Another activity could involve the use of shadow puppets like those used by the Java in Indonesia. Their Wayang shadow puppets are flat puppets usually made out of leather that are placed on banana stems. A storyteller moves the puppets around behind a white screen. The screen is lit from behind to cast shadows on the screen, which the audience watches.

Sensory Squares

Intended Ages

two years and older

Brain Connections

sensorimotor skills, expressive and receptive language, classifying

Materials Needed

- small textured items (buttons, leaf, twig, rock, cotton ball, paper clip, sandpaper, mirror)
- index card cut in half
- glue
- tape

Don't you sometimes wish you had something that could keep little hands busy while you prepare a snack or an activity? Try keeping hands busy and minds guessing with sensory squares.

Glue or tape different textured items on cards, and tape them to the bottom of the table where you eat meals or do crafts. Let children touch or feel the different textures and shapes (without being able to see what they are) while sitting and waiting for a new lesson to begin or for meals to arrive. Ask the children to identify what they are touching and talk about how they figured it out. Change the shapes frequently to keep the activity interesting.

Extension Activities

Let children create their own sensory squares from objects they find. They can try to guess not only what the object is but whether the sensory square they're touching is one that they themselves made.

Multisensory Explorations

Have children close their eyes and identify different sounds they hear in the room.

Diversity Adaptations

Include items that might be common in different countries, such as rice paper, bamboo, beads, or various types of fabric.

Secret Scents

Intended Ages

three years and older

Brain Connections

sensorimotor skills, classifying, expressive and receptive language

Materials Needed

- small canisters (yogurt containers with lids work well)
- sponges
- scented oils, such as orange, coffee, anise, and ginger
- marker
- scissors

What's that smell? Working with young children, you probably utter that phrase several times a day. In most cases you already have a good idea what made that scent; you just need to find who created it. After hours of smelling tempera paint and playdough (among other things), wouldn't your nose like a break with some more pleasant scents?

Place a small sponge inside each container to absorb the scents you add. Add enough drops to saturate the sponge or until you get a pretty good whiff of the odor. With the tip of a scissors, carefully poke a few holes in the lid, and label the bottom with the scent to double-check guesses.

Extension Activities

Experiment with smells to see if you can come up with familiar combinations, such as cinnamon roll or apple pie.

Multisensory Explorations

Put items that make sounds, such as rice or popcorn kernels, in the containers, and have the children guess what's inside.

Diversity Adaptations

Include scents from cultures that might not be familiar to all the children. For some children, this will be a learning experience. For others, the scents will be welcome and familiar.

Flash Cards

Intended Ages

four years and older

Brain Connections

comparing, creative thinking, sensorimotor skills

Materials Needed

- heavy paper such as card stock
- templates for shapes
- pencils
- scissors
- flashlight
- sheet or chart paper for screen (or a movie screen, if you have one)

These aren't your typical flash cards. These cards are shadow makers. When used with a flashlight in a dark room, the cards cast shadows on the wall.

Have children either draw their own shapes or use precut templates (dinosaurs, flowers, animals, numbers, shapes, child's name) to create shapes on the card stock. Cookie cutters or dough shape cutters would work as templates. Once the children have drawn the shape on the card, the shape will need to be cut out. You may have to help cut out the shapes so that they are closely trimmed without cutting the edge of the paper.

When the cards are ready, turn off the lights and shine the flashlights through the shapes on the screen. Screens can be blank walls without other visual distractions, a sheet or chart paper hanging on the wall to cover up the distractions, or an actual presentation screen if you have one.

Extension Activities

Use different types of paper to create the cutouts: the projected shape could be larger or smaller, have greater detail, or be more abstract. This would include using tissue paper to create different colors or add detail. Each child could also have a card with a different word or picture on it. Children could take turns holding up their shadow cards, and the group could make up a story about them.

Multisensory Explorations

Use different colors of lightbulbs in the flashlights to project the images in different colors. Play background music to help with the movement of the flashlights for a more sensory experience.

Diversity Adaptations

Use shapes and templates to illustrate different objects that might be found in different cultures, such as an igloo or a house on stilts.

ART

Brain Connections

Human beings have a basic need to express their emotions and thoughts. Often this happens through artistic expression. Music, movement, language, and emotion are all processed through the frontal lobe of the brain. Making connections in the frontal lobe helps develop executive function.

The work of young children is a natural art form. Playing, singing, drawing, and dancing are all forms of art. Cognitive areas of the brain are enhanced when children learn rhymes, experiment with drawing, and engage in social interactions with each other (Sousa 2006).

Art, like language, can be present in all activities. It's all how you look at it. Isn't beauty in the eye of the beholder? If you create a smokin' volcano, won't you think it's a work of art? Or how about completing a complex math assignment? Won't you be able to see the beauty in that bar graph? So many opportunities exist for adding an artistic flair to activities, but sometimes the focus needs to be on the actual process of making and building art for the sake of art itself.

You'll never hear me say that the final product is any more valuable than the process itself. In fact, the process is the only thing that matters to me. You would think I was trying to amass thousands of modeling clay dishes if you saw the ones I have been given by my children over the years. The truth is they serve only as reminders that children had the opportunity to hold the clay in their hands and feel the smooth, cool texture between their fingers. They were able to create something using their own thinking with their own purpose in mind. That is what makes these works of art beautiful to me. It's the journey, not the destination. Explore, create, be novel. Your brain will love you! It might even kiss you back!

Supporting Art in the Environment

Art is so open-ended that there is an endless supply of resources available at children's disposal. Not all resources are costly. In fact, in many cases, recycling and pilfering are the best ways to get art supplies. Here is a list of suggested materials, but feel free to add some interesting things of your own:

scissors	staplers	tape
rulers	chalk	rope
feathers	leaves	sponges
sandpaper	glue	glitter
buttons	paint (finger, tempera, acrylic)	paintbrushes
modeling clay	sticks	dirt
sand	paper of all kinds	markers
crayons	scissors	rocks
cardboard	tissue	cotton balls
straws	yarn	felt
fabric	Velcro fasteners	safety pins
pipe cleaners	tinfoil	foam pieces

(I could add to this list all day!)

Art and Infants

The first masterpiece a baby will admire will be your face. Nothing is more aesthetically pleasing to an infant than the human face. It's the child's keen sense of visual recognition that is at work here, and the more novel the object, the longer it will hold her attention. Given a choice between novel stimuli and familiar stimuli, the infant will chose the novel. A changing face (while familiar) can be a source of novelty with each changing expression. Think of your face as a canvas and the first piece of art a baby will appreciate.

An infant's visual perception is rapidly developing at this stage. Creating a visually stimulating environment will enhance this development. Change objects in the room frequently, or at least rotate their placement around the room. Continue to narrate as infants explore the environment, adding comments about aesthetics. Be specific about the qualities that deem something pleasing or not. Instead of just saying, "That's a pretty flower." Saying something like, "The colors and shape of this flower are so interesting to look at." This strengthens vocabulary and also helps children gain a sense of what qualities make something aesthetically pleasing. They will discover that beauty is in the eye of the beholder.

Infants can engage in art opportunities with older children in activities such as finger painting if you give them something like pudding to "paint" with. While safely secured in a high chair, a baby could use the tray as the paper and explore the feeling of the pudding between his fingers. He could squish it, smear it, wipe it—all things that will develop those fine-motor skills and begin the process of art creation!

Selecting Resource Books for Art

Children's books by their very nature could be considered art books. With their colorful illustrations, their stories seem to come alive. Not all art books are about art. There are plenty that describe the process of making art and what constitutes art, but for young children the main selection criteria should be the appeal a book has for young children. Is it aesthetically pleasing to them? Does the book reinforce vocabulary, the use of their senses, and appreciation for the physical world around them?

SUGGESTED BOOKS—AGES BIRTH TO FOUR

Anholt, Laurence. 2007. *Van Gogh and the sunflowers*. Hauppauge, NY: Barron's Educational Series.

Lionni, Leo. 1995. *Little blue and little yellow*. New York: HarperCollins.

Seuss, Dr. 1996. *My many colored days*. New York: Knopf Books for Young Readers.

Tafolla, Carmen. 2009. *What can you do with a rebozo?/¿Qué puedes hacer con un rebozo?* Illustrated by Amy Cordova. New York: Tricycle Press.

SUGGESTED BOOKS—AGES FIVE TO EIGHT

Anholt, Laurence. 2007. *Picasso and the girl with a ponytail*. Hauppauge, NY: Barron's Educational Series.

Brumbeau, Jeff. 2004. *The quilt maker's journey*. Illustrated by Gail de Marcken. New York: Scholastic.

Buehner, Caralyn. 2002. *Snowmen at night*. Illustrated by Mark Buehner. New York: Dial Press.

Polacco, Patricia. 1996. *Rechenka's eggs*. New York: Putnam Juvenile.

Homemade Scratch-and-Sniff Books

Intended Ages
four years and older

Brain Connections
sensorimotor skills, predicting, cause and effect, creative thinking

Materials Needed
- heavy paper, such as card stock
- stapler
- powdered drink mix
- water
- paintbrushes

One of my childhood memories involves scratch-and-sniff books. There was something about that little felt circle on a page that got me excited about smelling something new and interesting. Here is a way to create your own scented books.

Create a story with pictures that might be represented by a flavor of powdered drink mix, perhaps a bunch of grapes, cherries, or lemons.

Then mix a packet of powdered drink mix with two tablespoons of water to create a thick paint. Let children paint the pictures in the book with the mix, and allow them to dry. Later, when the children scratch the picture, they will be able to smell the scent.

Extension Activities
Try real produce to create the same scents. If you rub a real grape on the paper, does it smell like a grape?

Multisensory Explorations
Try this activity with textured paper, such as sandpaper. The added roughness of the paper will create a deeper sensory experience when scratched. Some fine-grade sandpaper will go through inkjet printers, or you can use a marker to draw the shape on the sandpaper.

Diversity Adaptations
Create scented paint using different spices.

What's in the Bag?

Intended Ages

three years and older

Brain Connections

predicting, flexible thinking, sensorimotor skills

Materials Needed

- paper bags
- feathers
- stickers
- cotton balls
- foam shapes
- fabric swatches
- small rocks
- small pieces of sponge

Usually we understand that good art activities allow children to self-select materials. We want open-ended projects that foster creativity. But what if we still want to foster creativity while not allowing the child to pick the materials? Would this activity still be considered open-ended? Give it a try, and find out!

Place a variety of art objects into enough paper bags to have one bag for each child.

Give each child a different bag, and ask him to make something with the items in the bag. Someone may ask if she has to use all the items. I'd say the more the better, but I want this activity to be open-ended, so I'd let the child decide. Watch what happens when the children let their creativity fly. Compare what they made with their supplies. How are they alike? How are they different?

Extension Activities

Put different articles in each bag, or put the same articles in each bag. See which is more interesting or who comes up with the most similar or different ideas.

Multisensory Explorations

Include a variety of sensory materials in each bag. Bumpy, smooth, soft, hard—try to get as many different tactile things as possible.

Diversity Adaptations

Include objects that might be common in various cultures, such as different types of tree bark, bird feathers, cloth, or fabric. Look for art books in the library that show pictures of art from different places around the world.

Doable Dough

Intended Ages

two years and older

Brain Connections

cause and effect, creative thinking, sensorimotor skills

Materials Needed

- two cups flour
- one cup salt
- one cup water
- four tablespoons cream of tartar
- two teaspoons vegetable oil
- food coloring
- large pot
- stirring spoon
- heat source
- roller
- tools for cutting (cookie cutters)
- containers

Forget that store-bought stuff. You can make your own dough and create your own kinds of art. It's totally *doughable*!

Children can take turns adding the ingredients (except food coloring) into a large pot. Then cook the ingredients over medium heat, stirring frequently until the mixture is smooth. Remove it from the heat, and allow it to cool. Place extra flour on the table if the dough is still a bit sticky, and give each child a large blob that they can begin kneading until smooth. Once the dough is the right consistency (not too stiff, not too sticky), add food coloring to create different colors of dough.

Children can pound, smash, squeeze, and roll the dough to their hearts' content. You can also give them tools to cut and shape the dough or cookie cutters or other shape cutters to make different shapes with the dough.

When you're finished with the activity, the dough needs to be placed in a resealable container so that it lasts at least several weeks. I give each child a resealable container to store her own dough, because some children like to mix all the colors and others like to keep them separate. I leave it up to them.

Extension Activities

Add scented things to the dough, such as coffee or cinnamon, curry, or other spices.

Multisensory Explorations

Adding coffee grounds or sand will create a textured dough. If it's not important that the dough be smooth, try it out.

Diversity Adaptations

One of my favorite lessons from *Can We Eat the Art? Incredible Edibles and Art You Can't Eat* by Paula Guhin describes an activity with Ashanti dolls. These dolls are adapted from Ghana's Ashanti culture. The Ashanti people make "akua-ba" dolls for childbearing women to wear around their necks. It is believed that the shape of the doll's head (oval for girls, square for boys, round for a wise baby) will aid in the delivery of healthy babies. Over time the tradition of using the dolls as good luck charms gave way to using art as a way of expressing their tribal heritage and passing it on to succeeding generations.

Have the children shape the doable dough into dolls; place them on wax paper, and allow them to dry for several days or bake in an oven for several hours at 200 degrees. You can pierce a hole in the top of the doll to craft a necklace, and the children can use tempera paint to decorate the dolls. Activities such as these are a good way to share culture heritage, but more important, they demonstrate how ancient crafts continue to flourish in modern cultures.

ART

Upside-Down Art

Intended Ages

three years and older

Brain Connections

sensorimotor skills, creative thinking, perceptual-motor skills

Materials Needed

- paper
- low table
- paint
- markers
- chalk
- tape
- paintbrushes

There must be something to painting upside down—just think Michelangelo. You may not get a Sistine Chapel out of it, but children will certainly enjoy the chance to paint under a table.

Attach large sheets of paper to the underside of a low table, and invite children to sit or lie under the table to write or paint upside down on the paper. After they finish, create an art gallery show, and have the artists talk about their creations.

Extension Activities

If you have a glass table, you might consider letting children paint directly on the glass. This creates two images—one image from the underside, while the child is upside down, and one from the top, where you can look down on the glass and see the reverse image. If you are outside, you may even see the shadow that the paint on the table creates on the ground.

Multisensory Explorations

Add texture to the paint with feathers, twigs, straw, sand, etc.

Diversity Adaptations

Paint with different substances, such as mud, or add different scents to the paint, such as spices.

Sand Painting with Salt

Intended Ages
four years and older

Brain Connections
patterning, creative thinking

Materials Needed
- table, canning, or kosher salt
- food coloring
- container with lid
- glue
- pencils
- paper

I love the beach and feeling the sand between my toes. My children make a habit of bottling sand each time they visit an ocean to save it as a souvenir. So far they have the Atlantic (from the Delaware shore and Miami Beach) and the Indian Ocean (from Mombasa, Kenya). They especially like to compare the colors of the sand from the different beaches. But creating sandscapes can be easier than touring the globe.

Before you begin, prepare your salt. Add several tablespoons of salt to a container with a lid, add four or five drops of food coloring, put on the lid, and shake vigorously for sixty seconds.

Have the children create designs or pictures on paper with pencils, and then have them apply glue to the lines. Next they can sprinkle the glue lines with the colored salt to create a sand (well, actually a salt) art masterpiece. Display the artwork in a "gallery."

Extension Activities
Add additional items, such as shells, feathers, leaves, flowers, etc.

Multisensory Explorations
Add scents to the salt, such as spices or powdered drink mix.

Diversity Adaptations
Use a variety of colors when tinting the salt. Use natural earth tones to allow children to create diverse images.

Pasta Pictures

Intended Ages
three years and older

Brain Connections
sensorimotor skills, creative thinking

Materials Needed
- dried pasta in different shapes and lengths
- construction paper
- glue
- pancils

This is a favorite classic activity but often overlooked today as more sophisticated materials come on the market for making art. I think this biodegradable art makes an equally nice picture collage.

Offer the children various sizes of pasta shapes so they can create a textured picture on a piece of construction paper. You can vary the size or shape of the paper. They can create collages as well. Ask the children to make self-portraits with different types of pasta such as bowtie pasta in a girl's hair, spaghetti for pigtails—you name it.

Depending on the creation desired, children can use pencils to predraw the pictures they want, or they can begin placing the pasta in whatever ways they want. Different patterns can be created to represent something important or of interest to the child. Anything is possible.

Extension Activities
Use other dried foods, such as lentils, rice, or beans, along with the pasta. (I would use rice to make freckles on my self-portrait.)

Multisensory Explorations
You can add dried onion or garlic flakes, basil, or parsley. These other foods and seasonings will provide color and scent.

Diversity Adaptations
Use materials that are common in different cultures. Beans, rice, and pasta are all staples in many diets and make fun art. But in some cultures food is so precious that using it on art projects is seen as wasteful. Be sure to have conversations with families about their views, or ask them to donate unused (otherwise discarded) dried, nonperishable foods as art supplies.

Stained-Glass Pictures

Intended Ages

three years and older

Brain Connections

creative thinking

Materials Needed

- roll of clear contact paper
- tissue paper (variety of colors)
- scissors
- tape or string

I love clear contact paper. The fact that it's not really "paper" is appealing to me. I like that I can stick whatever I want on it and see it on both sides.

Have children use scraps of colored tissue paper (because it's light and translucent) to create "stained-glass" pictures in between two sheets of clear contact paper. Have children select different pieces of colored tissue paper, and invite them to make different shapes by either cutting or tearing the paper. Different techniques will create different looks. Then give each child a sheet of contact paper with the backing peeled off. For younger children it's better to work with smaller sheets of contact paper, since they are very, very sticky! Once the artist has finished creating his or her masterpiece, remove the backing from a second piece of contact paper and very carefully place on top (sticky side to sticky side) of the picture. Because the paper is sticky, it is tricky to get it applied over the first sheet without any bubbles. If you do make a mistake putting the second piece of contact paper on the picture, consider just how badly you need to fix this. If it's a small wrinkle, you will more than likely damage the picture by trying to pull the two pieces of contact paper apart. If it's just a bubble, you can use a pencil to roll over it to squeeze out the air. Slight imperfections add to the beauty, so don't fret if the contact paper doesn't cover perfectly.

Once the pictures are complete, you can either tape them to windows to allow light to pass through or attach strings and hang them from the ceiling.

Extension Activities

Precut geometric shapes out of tissue paper for children to choose from when creating their stained-glass pictures.

Multisensory Explorations

Include objects from nature in the materials available for the project—leaves, feathers, twigs, flowers, etc.

Diversity Adaptations

Provide pictures or examples of geometric shapes and patterns found in textiles, architecture, art, and landscapes from various cultures. Encourage children to incorporate these patterns and designs into their pictures.

Bubble Paintings

Intended Ages

two years and older

Brain Connections

creative thinking, predicting, cause and effect

Materials Needed

- shallow dish
- cardboard or mat board
- straws
- liquid dish soap
- tempera paint

Children love painting, and they love bubbles. What about combining the two?

Place one-quarter cup of tempera paint and two squirts of liquid dish soap in a shallow dish. Have children use straws to blow bubbles into the paint. When the bubbles get to the surface, place the mat board or cardboard on top of the dish (allowing the straw to stick out the side). Have the children continue to blow bubbles to transfer the paint from the bubbles onto the cardboard.

The strength of the bubbles blown will determine how much paint gets applied to the mat board. After a minute or two of blowing, the child can slowly pull the mat board off to see if she likes the picture the bubbles have made. If she does, she can turn it over and allow it to dry. If not, she can keep blowing!

Extension Activities

Use different types of paper (construction, newsprint), fabric, or canvas to see how the paint and bubbles respond to different surfaces.

Multisensory Explorations

If the dish soap is not already scented, try adding different scents from spices or powdered drink mix to create distinct smells. Or try different scents of soap, such as lemon or lavender. Scents will vary from brand to brand, so you may have to try several before you find the one that works best. Add glitter or sequins to the finished picture to create texture.

Diversity Adaptations

Use different textiles or types of paper found in different cultures to use as the canvas for the bubble picture.

Drawing in the Dark

Intended Ages
three years and older

Brain Connections
observing, perceptual-motor skills, predicting

Materials Needed
- paper
- markers or crayons*

*Children will be writing in the dark and may miss their paper or go off the edges. Be careful to choose writing tools that won't damage the writing surface should the child repeatedly miss the paper.

Have you ever tried closing your eyes to conjure up images or prompt your memory? What is it about the dark that helps you use your imagination? Well, for one thing, the darkness removes visual stimuli. Removing visual distractions can help the artist rely on his memory (or imagination) to fuel his creativity. And removing one sense allows the other senses to do a bit of overtime and flex their muscles.

Have children select writing tools and paper. When children are seated at the table with the paper and markers or crayons, turn off the lights, and ask them to think of a specific memory. "Can you remember the first time you ate ice cream? Do you remember how you felt?" After helping them conjure up a memory, ask them to draw a picture about this memory. (For example, a picture of an ice cream cone or of them eating it.)

You don't always have to ask them to have a memory, but you can try giving them prompts if they seem stuck.

Extension Activities
Cover the entire table with one sheet of paper, and have all the children draw on the paper, making a large collage. You could even have each child dictate what her picture is about, while you write the words on the paper.

Multisensory Explorations
Offer different types of paper children can touch, such as rough sandpaper or other textured paper. Use scented markers to engage olfactory processing. Play different types of music to create different moods as children draw.

Diversity Adaptations
Share stories with children about how light sources are different across the planet. Some homes use electricity, but others use candles or solar power. Some places have darkness for longer periods of time (and conversely shorter periods of daylight). Share ideas about how children may adapt to different light sources over time. How would it affect their playtime? How would it affect their schooling? It is interesting to discover how children feel about this, since being afraid of the dark is a common fear. Creating opportunities to experience darkness in a positive way may help ease some children's fears.

ART

MOTOR SKILLS

Brain Connections

Movement is deeply linked to cognitive learning, and exercise improves memory. If you engage children in movement during learning, and you are able to involve both hemispheres, children are likely to have greater recall of information. If children read a story, they will remember a piece of the information that is presented in the language-processing center in the left hemisphere. However, children will be able to remember ideas in whole chunks (not just the sum of the parts) if they use both hemispheres. They are more likely to remember the story if they hear the story being read, clap out the syllables, and have a chance to write or draw their own story or illustrations (Sousa 2006).

The cerebellum, primarily responsible for motor function, is also connected by nerve fiber to the frontal lobe, which is responsible for cognitive functions. Research is discovering that learning about movement improves our understanding of its link to learning and memory (Sousa 2006).

Have you heard (or even said yourself) that if we could bottle the energy of children, we could reduce our dependency on all other forms of energy? They seem to have an endless supply. Sadly, we can't bottle it, so we have to help them expend it to make sure they don't bottle it up inside themselves and eventually explode.

Motor skills help children not only expend energy but also send that energy to their brains. Exercise and movement prompt the liver to create glucose, which provides energy to the brain, leading to memory formation. Although this section provides specific activities designed around motor skills, keep in mind the value of movement in memory formation, and include movement whenever possible in all activities children engage in. (Remember: the brain cannot absorb what the butt cannot endure.) Now get moving!

Supporting Motor Skills in the Environment

You don't really need too many specific things to practice motor skills, but having the right kind of objects available can make it a lot more fun. In addition to your own favorites, include some of these items in your environment:

- balls
- jump ropes
- wheels
- balance beam
- parachutes
- streamers
- climbing things
- scissors
- puzzles
- manipulatives
- shovels and scoops
- pencils and markers

Infants and Motor Skills

Movement is critical to infant brain development. Rocking a baby does more than provide emotional comfort (although that is necessary for brain-based learning too); it stimulates the vestibular region of the inner ear. This region is responsible for language development.

While it's vital to place a baby on her back to sleep, tummy time (also called floor play) is equally vital when she is awake. Always provide supervision, but give infants as much time in unrestricted movement as possible. Nothing builds motor development like being able to kick, scoot, wiggle, and shimmy. Create sensory tubes (plastic bottles with different objects in them, such as rice, beans, or marbles—make sure you hot-glue or super-glue those lids on!) that babies can roll on the floor. Once babies start to crawl, they can push and roll the bottles across the room. Just think of all the cause-and-effect connections being made!

Selecting Books and Resources for Motor Skills

It's a good thing children love to move and groove, because there are plenty of books to support motor skills. Look for books that demonstrate healthy attitudes toward exercise, that encourage movement throughout the story, or that involve acting out the story.

SUGGESTED BOOKS—AGES BIRTH TO FOUR

Asch, Frank. 2008. *Like a windy day*. Orlando: Voyager Books.

Ormerod, Jan. 2007. *Whoosh around the mulberry bush*. Oxford: Oxford University Press.

Roberts, Sheena. 2004. *We all go traveling by*. Cambridge, MA: Barefoot Books.

Stockland, Patricia M. 2005. *Swing, slither, or swim: A book about animal movement*. Mankato, MN: Picture Window Books.

SUGGESTED BOOKS—AGES FIVE TO EIGHT

Blackstone, Stella. 2006. *Walking through the jungle*. Cambridge, MA: Barefoot Books.

Dahl, Michael. 2003. *Do goldfish gallop? A book about animal movement*. Mankato, MN: Picture Window Books.

Gruetzke, Mary. 2005. *There were ten in the bed*. New York: Scholastic.

Ryder, Joanne. 1999. *Earthdance*. New York: Henry Holt.

Follow the Language Leader

Intended Ages

three years and older

Brain Connections

sensorimotor skills, expressive and receptive language

Materials Needed

- a variety of objects from around the room

This activity is "Telephone" meets "Follow the Leader."

Make a list of objects around the room that can have more than one name or have different names from what you normally use to describe the objects. For example, your list might include:

couch = sofa

window = glass

door = entrance

shelf = sill

floor = ground

carpet = floor covering

ball = sphere

Tell the children they are going on a word hunt, and invite them to follow the language leader. Start by leading the line of children around the room. Stop at certain objects, point to them, and give two different names for each object. Have the first child repeat the two names to the next child. That child repeats them to the next and so on and so on, until all children in the line have said the different names of the object. Remember, practice makes permanent. When each child has to repeat the word, she has the chance to practice it, which will work to make it permanent in her memory. It's a fun way to demonstrate synonyms and build vocabulary.

Extension Activities

Give children each a turn at being the leader. Use expressive language to describe the items, and encourage the children to make new selections each round.

Multisensory Explorations

Blindfold the children, and pass an object along to each of them. Have them feel it, say what they think it is, and pass it along to the next child. Once the item reaches the end of the line, have the children take off their blindfolds. Discuss what the item really is.

Diversity Adaptations

Try the same activity, but use a word in a different language, such as Spanish, Farsi, Swahili, or American Sign Language.

Obstacle Course, of Course

Intended Ages
one year and older

Brain Connections
problem solving, creative thinking

Materials Needed
- physical items to create an obstacle course, such as chairs, tumble mat, sheet over chairs to create tunnel, hoops to crawl/jump through, ladder, step stool, etc.

Never underestimate the value of creating challenging obstacle courses for children of all ages. Demonstrating concepts like over and under, around and through, up and down, inside and outside can be experienced through climbing courses.

Create an obstacle course for children of diverse skills and abilities to navigate. The ages of the children should determine how complex you make the course. While children navigate the course, they work on problem solving, motor skills, and team building, depending on the complexity of the course. The more cognitively challenging, the more chances there are for rehearsal of these skills. Making the course physically challenging can also provide exercise and gross-motor development.

Extension Activities
You could have schoolagers create their own course that requires teamwork: they all successfully complete the course, or they all have to start over.

Multisensory Explorations
Try to add novelty to the experience by having children go through the course silently or use blindfolds. Once finished, have the group debrief to talk about the parts they liked best or what the hardest challenges were.

Diversity Adaptations
Not all children have the same physical abilities as other children the same age, whether they have physical challenges or not. Some children will have more defined upper body strength or fine-motor skills—obstacle courses can help children build on their existing skills and develop new strengths as well. If you have a child who is differently-abled, be mindful about creating an obstacle course that could be adapted for a child in a wheelchair or other adaptive device. You could also create a course that demonstrates a different geographical location, such as a desert or a jungle. Depending on how messy you want to get, you could use a baby pool to hold a layer of sand to create a sand pit, and you could have ropes or ribbons suspended (from the ceiling, taped to the bottom of a table or chair, etc.) that children walk or crawl through to create a feeling of a jungle or rain forest. Add music to help create the sensory feeling of another place. You could use sounds like wind blowing in the desert or tropical animals chattering in the rain forest.

MOTOR SKILLS

Pass the Pretzel, Please

Intended Ages

five years and older

Brain Connections

creative thinking, problem solving

Materials Needed

- chopsticks or small dowels
- large pretzel or circular object

Cooperation is a vital social skill children need in order to get along with one another. In our competitive world, it can be hard to help children find prosocial ways to build a team. This activity is a fun way to get children working together without competition.

Give each child a chopstick. Have all children line up (or stand in a circle), and have them pass the pretzel from one child to the next using only the chopsticks. It might sound easy, but it can be quite challenging to balance the pretzel on the stick and slide it off to the other child's stick without using hands. Children will gain problem-solving skills as they work on their fine-motor skills.

Extension Activities

Add music, and have the children continue passing until the music stops, similar to "Musical Chairs."

Multisensory Explorations

Try blindfolding the children to add sensory complexity.

Diversity Adaptations

Instead of passing the pretzel, use another object, such as a bagel, large bead, or wooden bracelet.

R Is for Reverse

Intended Ages
three years and older

Brain Connections
flexible thinking, perceptual-motor skills

Materials Needed
none

Before I learned to drive, my dad always joked that the *R* on the car's gear shift stood for *race*. When he was teaching me to drive, I joked with him that I still believed that. For some reason he didn't think that was funny anymore!

Have children try doing their normal routines while walking in reverse. Obviously you need to have them do this safely, but they can still have fun! Challenge children to do this throughout the day—going to the bathroom to wash up for lunch, heading out to the playground, coming together for circle time, etc. This activity helps create improved spatial awareness and re-creates a visual memory of the actual route.

Extension Activities
Instead of walking backward, have children try switching from dominant hand to nondominant hand to complete a task. For children who are writing, have them write backward. Children who can count could count backward from five to one or ten to one.

Multisensory Explorations
Have children write a letter backward, and have another child use a mirror to read it.

Diversity Adaptations
Not all languages are read the way English is (from left to right). Some languages are read from right to left (such as Hebrew and Arabic) or from starting at the back (meaning the spine is on the right instead of the left) and working forward, like Japanese. And Chinese is read bottom to top. Try having the children write stories in a different direction. Or read a story to children moving from right to left and see if they can still figure out the story.

Balance Beam

Intended Ages

two years and older

Brain Connections

cause and effect, perceptual-motor skills

Materials Needed

- six-inch- or eight-inch-diameter PVC pipe, eight feet long
- T-shaped connector joints for the ends
- pipe glue, if necessary, to hold connectors in place
- Velcro strips (optional foot grips)
- protective padding

I got this idea from my good buddy Jeff A. Johnson in his book *Do-It-Yourself Early Learning* (2006). It's so good, it's worth borrowing. I coerced my husband, Josh, into coming with me to the local home improvement store. He was reluctant when I told him I needed an eight-foot-long piece of PVC pipe. "What for?" he wanted to know. At the store, I selected a choice pipe and placed it on the floor to test whether it could support my weight. (Amazingly, it could, so I wanted to take it home with me if for no other reason than that.) "Ah, a balance beam," he said. "You'll need to connect a cross piece on each end for support so it doesn't roll. Here, these T-joints will work." And right there in aisle 8 our balance beam was born.

Create your own large balance beam out of six-inch or eight-inch PVC pipe. Cut two feet off the end of your eight-foot pipe, and then cut that piece into four more equal pieces. Add con-nector T-joints on each end of the long pipe, and insert the cut pieces into each end of the T-joints to form a giant letter *I*. It's a good idea to glue these *T* connectors together for safety so the pipe doesn't roll with a child walking on it. But if the pieces fit together snugly (and they often do), don't limit your resources by gluing the connec-tors. You may find another purpose for that giant pipe. Fasten strips of Velcro (sticky side up) on the beam to add grip.

Have children practice walking across the beam. Place it between two very low chairs, and include it in a larger obstacle course to allow children to climb over or under the beam. If you do choose to elevate it (I recommend only a few inches), use protective padding below the beam, and make sure it doesn't roll or slide off the ele-vated surface.

In addition to the way I suggested using the balance beam above, my kids have been able to use the giant *I*, as they call it, for a variety of pur-poses. They incline it against the couch and stick an arm through the cross piece to where they can reach the center tunnel, and they drop balls, cars, Legos, and pretty much anything that will slide down the tube to see which end of the bottom cross support the object will come out. They also slide down the beam when it's inclined against the couch like a very slanted firefighter's pole.

Extension Activities

Even if the T-joints are glued in place, the open pipe can serve as a ball shoot when elevated. Children can become good predictors even when they can't see how the ball (mini car, Lego, just about anything small!) is going to come out the other end of the pipe.

Multisensory Explorations

You can have the children walk barefoot on the Velcro to feel the bumpy texture or in socks on the smooth side to slip around.

Diversity Adaptations

Engage children in thinking about ways an object like this balance beam would come in handy in their lives. Would a child in another country need something like a beam to get over a stream (like a footbridge), or what about a rope bridge in the jungle? How many different parts of the world use bridges to connect people with places they want to go? You could make a different kind of bridge together, such as a small footbridge out of wood, and use it in your dramatic play area. This would be a good project activity that could unfold over time.

MOTOR SKILLS

Walking the Walk and Talking the Talk

Intended Ages

three years and older

Brain Connections

perceptual-motor skills, expressive and receptive language, creative thinking

Materials Needed

Some days I just don't feel like myself. Instead, I feel like a ballet dancer or an auctioneer. Maybe children have the same urge to be someone else for a change. Have children move about their day in silly ways. You have to get from point A to point B anyway—why not make it interesting?

Is Sam heading to the sink to wash his hands? Have him walk like a cowboy from the old West. Is Sonya heading out to the playground? See if she can move like a Russian dancer kicking out her feet. Are you listening to some music and feeling the mood to dance? Get in a line, arm in arm, and tap dance over to the table for lunch. Creating novelty is important for the brain, and it primes it for what is coming next. Having children move in novel ways wakes up both hemi-spheres and gets the brain fired up for what comes next, like problem solving or lunch! It can be fun, and it can exercise muscles. It's a win-win proposition.

Extension Activities

There are lots of ways to add novelty to the day's routines. Change your voice or persona as you go about your day. Got a good Elvis impersonation? How about that British accent you like to practice? Children love this sort of "entertainment," and it's good for their brains!

Multisensory Explorations

Add music that is created by things other than instruments (rushing water, thunderstorms, wind, animal calls) to fit the kind of dance move or emotion you are going for.

Diversity Adaptations

Take advantage of this activity to help children develop an appreciation for world music by playing a variety of music, which could include bagpipes, wind chimes, penny whistles, kalimbas, and drums.

Animals on the Move

Intended Ages
two years and older

Brain Connections
creative thinking, perceptual-motor skills, observing

Materials Needed
none

You know the saying "It's a jungle out there." Well, most days, it's a jungle in here too!

Have children choose an animal they like. Invite them to move as that animal and make its sounds. Children can choose to sort themselves by similar animal characteristics or try to figure out what kinds of animals their friends are. Children can develop an ability to infer (reach logical conclusions) based on what they already know about animals and how the group is behaving.

Extension Activities
Create masks to represent the types of animals being acted out.

Multisensory Explorations
Play songs such as "The Lion Sleeps Tonight," "Old MacDonald Had a Farm," "Waltzing with Bears," "Going to the Zoo," and other songs that promote playful animal acting.

Diversity Adaptations
Suggest a wide range of types of animals for children to be, especially animals found in other countries. How about a water buffalo, kangaroo, llama, or penguin?

MOTOR SKILLS

What's Cookin'?

Intended Ages

four years and older

Brain Connections

creative thinking, perceptual-motor skills

Materials Needed

I got this idea from a drama competition I participated in when I was in the sixth grade. One of my classmates performed in the mime category: he did a dramatic interpretation of a slice of bacon cooking without the sizzle. It was hard to know what he was doing because he wasn't allowed to make noise. Without hearing him sizzle, we assumed he was break dancing (it was the '80s, after all).

This got me thinking: Have you ever watched bacon sizzle or popcorn pop? What about gelatin jiggle or corn stand up tall? I knew children would have ideas about this.

Have children take the form of fruits and vegetables and act out a play as that food. Have each child teach his movement to the rest of the group. Whatever movement that child decides is appropriate for that item is what you go with. After all, who really knows how a head of lettuce would sway? We want children to make connections between their prior learning and their new

learning, but if they've never acted like lettuce before, they may not have this knowledge. They will have to make predictions, infer behavior, and be flexible thinkers. Sounds like a brain workout to me!

Extension Activities

Have the children combine similar types of food into groups or plan a meal with foods that complement each other based on the roles they are playing and acting out.

Multisensory Explorations

Have the children use materials to create a model of their food choice out of dough or paper for further exploration and role-playing.

Diversity Adaptations

Introduce a variety of food to children from various cultures so they have plenty of food choices to pretend to be. Try introducing passion fruit, plantains, tofu, egg rolls, or maize if these are unfamiliar to some children. Survey the children and learn about foods that are familiar to them and use these food choices in ways that can help children learn about each other. Look for the similarities in choices and introduce new foods along with familiar ones to demonstrate how many foods complement each other.

Who Am I?

Intended Ages

five years and older

Brain Connections

deductive reasoning, perceptual-motor skills, observing

Materials Needed

- pictures or words of animals, objects, places, or people on large index cards
- tape

Have children form a circle, and then attach a card to the back of each child. Depending on the reading level of the children, you may choose to use pictures instead of written words. Then, without the children knowing what is on the cards on their backs, they must go around to the other children and ask them yes or no questions about the cards. One might ask, "Am I an animal?" The other child will answer only yes or no, and they take turns asking. Each pair gets to ask only one question at a time. After each person in that pairing has asked one question, each rotates to another child and proceeds to ask one more question. Depending on the size of the group, children may rotate to new pairings several times before they figure out what they are. Once a child knows what is on the card on her back, she can step out of the circle. This activity can be a lot of fun, and it's also helping to craft good deductive reasoning skills. The interaction is good social practice, and language skills are enhanced as children work to find ways to describe what they think is on the cards.

Extension Activities

Give the game a twist: Play a round where this time the child knows what he is, but when he pairs up with another child, that child has to guess what he is by one clue that the child can give. Children must ask three other children for clues before repeating the process with any child. (This activity is meant to reinforce "Ask three before me.") Once everyone knows what all the children are, the game ends.

Multisensory Explorations

Use a combination of the above activities to enhance the game into a multisensory experience. Instead of using cards, children can select from a box of props that help demonstrate what they are. The children sit in a circle with their eyes closed, and one child at a time passes his object around the circle. Each child can ask one question without looking at the object. The child who chose the object only answers yes or no until someone is ready to guess.

Diversity Adaptations

When playing the game with the multisensory exploration, you could include objects, people, or animals that are common to children's home culture. Include scents or other objects that may be found in homes from diverse cultural backgrounds.

MOTOR SKILLS

Back-to-Back Ball

Intended Ages

six years and older

Brain Connections

convergent thinking, problem solving, perceptual-motor skills

Materials Needed

- one medium-size basketball or soccer ball for each pair of children

This game involves some good old-fashioned teamwork to get the ball rolling—well, actually not rolling so much as just moving. Before you begin, designate a start and finish line for the race. Have children pair up with a partner and stand back to back. Each pair holds a ball in place with their backs. (My daughter Elyse suggests squatting, as it makes it easier to move). With one player facing forward and the other facing backward, have the children race to the finish line without dropping the ball. Once the children reach the finish line, they return to the start line without turning around. The person who was facing backward now gets to face forward and vice versa.

The first leg of the race has the backward-facing child following directions and struggling to keep pace with the forward-facing child. When the roles are reversed, each child can experience what the other was feeling during the first leg.

The race is repeated as many times as there are pairs to run. You can pick your goal: fastest time, least amount of dropped balls, racing against another pair, etc. This kind of teamwork

helps form social connections and also gets the brain motivated by cross-lateral integration. By changing roles, the players use both hemispheres of their brains to integrate the skills rehearsed by the activity.

Extension Activities

There are different ways to encourage the children to move with the balls between their backs. They could play a game like "Red Light, Green Light," in which the pairs begin at the start line and wait to move until a caller shouts out, "Green light." The children walk together until the caller shouts out, "Red light," at which point they stop before the caller catches them moving. If they are caught, they have to return to the start line. If they don't get caught, they continue to repeat this process until they make it to the finish line without dropping the ball.

Multisensory Explorations

Instead of using a regular soccer or basketball, try using a ball with a bumpy surface. Children can feel the different textures on their backs as they squeeze the ball with a partner. Just be careful that the surface isn't uncomfortable.

Another way to have the children use more of their bodies is to play the race part of the game by having each child move in a crab-walk position. Children have their feet and hands on the ground (hands behind them, so their torsos are facing the sky). Each child moves like a crab, kicking the soccer ball to a stopping point, then returns and passes the ball off to another child. Or the children could play the game like soccer but as crabs. There can be many variations using more contact with their bodies for a multisensory (and cross-lateral) experience.

Diversity Adaptations

Sports receive different attention in different parts of the world. Soccer is actually called "football" in most other countries, and in Latin America soccer is as popular as football is in the United States. Talk with children about what other kinds of sports use balls and teamwork. Are the games played the same way in our country as they are in other countries? Do they use the same parts of their bodies? Do boys and girls play the games the same way?

SOCIAL-EMOTIONAL DEVELOPMENT

Brain Connections

Working with very young children to develop strong executive function and self-regulation will lead to positive social interaction and emotional well-being.

Children learn about the world around them through social contact and the development of relationships. By developing social wellness, children are able to form positive relationships and develop empathy and trust—all features developed in the limbic system, which is closely connected to our frontal lobe, where executive function takes place.

Children need to be able to develop strong executive function, which leads to self-regulation, which is paramount to developing healthy relationships with adults and other children. Relationships are the key to building healthy social-emotional intelligence, so when adults are able to use positive language, practice attunement, and be present in the moment with children, they aid in building healthy relationships.

The Center on the Social and Emotional Foundations for Early Learning is the go-to place for information on this topic. Visit www.vanderbilt. edu/csefel for an extensive selection of excellent resources for early childhood professionals as well as parents.

Supporting Social-Emotional Development in the Environment

Unlike other domain areas in this book, social-emotional development does not necessarily require any specific tools or materials. What it requires is a safe and healthy environment, which you will have already created by following chapter 2 to set up a brain-based learning environment.

The only thing to add is ensuring that children have their own personal spaces and that those spaces include comfy furniture, blankets to snuggle, and quiet areas.

Social-Emotional Development and Infants

For brain-based learning to be effective, environments need to be free from threats. Very young children need *more* than just an absence of threats—they need repeated and prolonged contact with a caring adult. Infants need to feel safe in a way that often can only be achieved by human contact. Holding and rocking an infant are very important for positive emotional development, but so are things like making eye contact and verbalizing reassurances, such as "Ms. Nikki is going to wash her hands. She'll be right back." "Look, I came back just as I said." "Here I am. I'm right here."

Social-emotional development is not as easy to see as other skills, such as when a child learns to walk or talk. You may not be sure about the results in this domain of development, but trust the process. Be understanding and patient during this time of self-discovery for infants. Keep routines consistent. This lets babies know they can predict what's going to happen next. That can help them feel secure. Use books and words that are common in a child's home language. Laminate pictures of family members, or use a photo book to allow babies to see throughout the day the smiling faces of people they love. I have this saying that I try to live by: the most important thing you can do when working with young children is to be consistent. And that is the hardest thing to do—being consistently consistent. You have to do what you say you are going to do. If you say you are going to be there for the baby, then be there for the baby.

Selecting Books for Social-Emotional Development

Books that support social-emotional development include those discussing how to be a friend, how to accept different friends, feelings (happiness, sadness, anger, fear, empathy), problem solving, and self-esteem.

SUGGESTED BOOKS—AGES BIRTH TO FOUR

Bang, Molly. 2006. *When Sophie gets angry—really, really, angry*. New York: Scholastic Audio Books.

Lionni, Leo. 2006. *A color of his own*. New York: Knopf Books for Young Readers.

Mayer, Mercer. 2000. *I was so mad*. New York: Random House Books for Young Readers.

Metzger, Steve. 2002. *I'll always come back!* New York: Scholastic.

SUGGESTED BOOKS—AGES FIVE TO EIGHT

Dewdney, Anna. 2007. *Llama llama mad at Mama*. New York: Viking Juvenile Books.

Henkes, Kevin. 2001. *Wemberly worried*. New York: Greenwillow Books.

Kissinger, Katie. 1994. *All the colors we are: The story of how we get our skin color*. St. Paul: Redleaf Press.

Munson, Derek. 2000. *Enemy pie*. San Francisco: Chronicle Books.

Silhouette Self-Portrait

Intended Ages
four years and older

Brain Connections
creative thinking, sensorimotor skills, observing

Materials Needed
- large sheets of paper
- overhead projector or other light projection source
- art materials (crayons, markers, stickers, glue, construction paper, yarn, fabric swatches)

Young children begin to form their identities based on what they feel on the inside long before it's evident on the outside. Having children create visual representations of their self-image helps build self-esteem and confidence. Two children can help each other with drawing the silhouette (if age appropriate), which builds interpersonal and peer collaboration skills.

Using an overhead projector (or other light source), capture a child's silhouette on a large piece of paper. After all the children's silhouettes are drawn on the paper, the children can decorate their self-portraits any way they choose. Create a space where all the silhouettes can be displayed.

This is an excellent project to do at least two times a year. When the second portrait is completed, pull out the first portrait and compare the two. Have the children look for differences in their own work. Ask them to describe ways in which they think they have changed over time.

Extension Activities
Either through dictation or by writing it themselves, have children create a story about how they came to be this person they have drawn. Ask them to describe what they were feeling while they were creating. Have them stand in front of their peers and use their words to describe their pictures to others.

Multisensory Explorations
Include various textures of art materials for children to create their self-image with. This could include sand, raised paint, buttons, fabric, etc.

Diversity Adaptations
Include different colors of paper for individuals to choose from. Include stickers or fabric swatches of different ethnic varieties (examples include African kente cloth, Native American weavings, Asian fabric swatches, etc.).

Pass the Face

Intended Ages
five years and older

Brain Connections
perceptual-motor skills, comparing

Materials Needed
none

This activity follows the same concept as the game of "Telephone," but "Pass the Face" transfers expressions instead of words.

Have the children sit in a circle. One child begins by making a face that shows an emotion such as happiness, sadness, anger, fear, etc. The child turns to her right and makes the face. That person makes the same face back to the first person and then turns and makes the face to the person to his right. Each child passes the face around the circle to the right until everyone has a chance to make the expression. Ask the children what each expression means. Follow with different expressions, with a different child beginning each time.

Extension Activities
Make the expression more complex by including sounds and gestures. A frustrated face might be accompanied by "Urgh!" and fists in the air. A sad face might include pretend wiping of tears and sounds of sobbing.

Multisensory Explorations
Encourage children to work with a partner and sit face to face. Have one child make an expression on her face while the other child closes his eyes and uses his hands to touch his partner's face to try to determine what kind of an expression she is making.

Diversity Adaptations
Some facial expressions are universal, such as smiling and frowning, crying and cheering, and the look of fear. But some people in different cultures might use their expressions to communicate in other ways. Ask families to share histories, or do some research to find out some of these cultural differences and share them with the children.

SOCIAL-EMOTIONAL

What's All the Hoopla?

Intended Ages
three years and older

Brain Connections
flexible thinking, observing, perceptual-motor skills

Materials Needed
- hula hoops (or other similar ringed objects)

Give children the freedom to move about in their own spaces. It helps them develop an understanding of other people's personal space and their movement in relation to others' movements.

Use a hula hoop on the floor to help children get a visual idea of the amount of personal space they have that no one else can impose on. To demonstrate when sharing is not appropriate, children can practice having toys or their personal materials in their own circle that are off-limits to other children. This kind of visual reminder helps children gain a sense of boundaries and respect for personal space. It also builds trust that children won't come and swipe a toy before a child is finished with it.

Extension Activities
Children practice a "space walk" by holding the hula hoop to see how much space is usually appreciated between people. This helps define the concept of the *personal bubble* that is common in Western culture.

Multisensory Explorations
Play music to allow children to dance holding their hoops or actually do hula hooping.

Diversity Adaptations
Engage children in a conversation about how different cultures adhere to different social standards about personal space. Some cultures enjoy close proximity, and others need even more than what we might be used to.

Mood Mask

Intended Ages
four years and older

Brain Connections
problem solving, observing

Materials Needed
- paper plates
- string
- markers
- scissors
- pictures of facial expressions

Remember the old song "Put on a Happy Face"? Some days when I'm working with cranky kids, I wish it were that easy. But this activity can help children learn to self-regulate their emotions by letting them see what they look like happy.

Create masks by using paper plates with strings attached to the sides for tying around children's heads. Have children create different faces on the masks to display a variety of emotions. Show children pictures of people making different kinds of expressions. Provide materials to allow children to create masks for as many different kinds of expressions they would like. Children can take turns wearing the masks and acting out the associated emotions. By rehearsing different emotions, children can learn how to self-regulate and control their emotions. Talk with children about appropriate ways to deal with feelings, and talk about how they feel when they are experiencing different moods.

Extension Activities
Create masks with pictures of the child making different expressions. You can use pictures you take with a digital camera. Print out the picture on card stock large enough to cover a child's face. Attach strings on the side, and be sure to create eye holes. Once a child begins to understand what feelings are, when she feels like expressing herself, she can don the appropriate mask.

Multisensory Explorations
A variety of materials can be used to make personalized masks that have textured hair, scented perfume, or other features. Consider using recycled items such as bottle caps or separated six-pack beverage rings for features like eyes or cheeks.

Diversity Adaptations
Include materials to represent different hair types and skin tones if making masks to represent actual children.

Puppets as People

Intended Ages
three years and older

Brain Connections
creative thinking, receptive and expressive language

Materials Needed
- gloves or mittens
- paper
- decorations (eyes, eyelashes, buttons, yarn, ribbon, sequins)
- glue, or hot glue (if necessary)
- sticks

Puppets are great tools for helping young children safely express issues that might be bothering them. We are used to making paper bag puppets, but what about glove puppets? Try taking the familiar and making it more novel. Provide materials to allow children to make their own puppet, and when they are finished, the children will have special friends and newfound voices.

Give each child a glove or mitten and allow children to decorate the puppets to the extent they can. Be prepared to assist younger children with gluing (and maybe even hot-gluing, depending on the fabric used) or sewing on facial features. Provide a variety of materials they can use to decorate the fingertips that will allow children to use these new friends to tell stories. Children could also make paper puppets that slip right on their fingers. Be creative and provide yarn for hair, strings for eyelashes, googly eyes, and other materials to enable children to make unique puppets that may help them express themselves in a way that diffuses anxiety. Puppetry also creates symbolic play, which allows children to try out different problem-solving skills.

Extension Activities
Allow children to attach their puppets to craft sticks or dowels, or to make marionettes hanging from strings. They can use puppets to act out a dramatic play using either predesigned scripts or open-ended dialogue.

Multisensory Explorations
Select a wide variety of textured fabrics, different types of paper, and buttons that are rough or smooth for children to choose from. Add plastic, foam, or shiny objects to decorate the puppets.

Diversity Adaptations
Provide materials for creating puppets with features that represent various ethnicities, cultures, or nationalities.

Tude O'Meter

Intended Ages

five years and older

Brain Connections

expressive and reflective language, critical thinking

Materials Needed

- construction paper
- markers
- butterfly clasps
- clothespins

Designed to reflect a child's current attitude, the tude o'meter helps children learn to regulate their emotions.

Give the children five pieces of paper to make faces. Have them draw a circle on each piece of paper. On each circle the children can draw an expression of anger, sadness, happiness, or something else. Give each child a clothespin. The children can decorate the circles and their clothespins (labeled with their names) however they'd like. Attach clasps to the five completed circles and hang them on the wall in an area accessible to the children. Children can move their clothespins to the corresponding mood as their moods change during the day. (I recommend laminating the circles to make them more durable.)

If a child is involved in an altercation with another child and he gets angry, he can come to the tude o'meter and move his clip from happy to angry. In doing this, the child removes himself from the situation and takes a break from the toxic atmosphere that led to the misunderstanding. This step helps a child recover from the bad feeling much faster than if he did nothing at all. Later, if he's happy, he can move his clip again so he show others that his mood has changed.

Extension Activities

Create a circular meter like a clock face, with small circles representing each mood of a child arranged around the inside perimeter of a big circle (where the numbers on a clock would be). Attach an arrow at the center of the large circle. On each small circle attach a digital photo of the child making an expression for each mood. The child can then move the arrow to the appropriate photo during the day to share her feelings.

Multisensory Explorations

You could attach small bells to the tude o'meter, or you could even use a wind chime to create a mood spectrum, attaching small pieces of paper to the chime indicating happy on the high-note end and sad on the low-note end. Children then move the chime or ring the bell to indicate their mood.

Diversity Adaptations

Use a variety of materials to decorate the meter to reflect colors and symbolism from diverse children's cultures.

SOCIAL-EMOTIONAL

Going on a Trip

Intended Ages

six years and older

Brain Connections

matching, sequencing, creative thinking

Materials Needed

My dad used to get us to play this game on long car rides to keep us from nagging him about whether we were there yet. This game is a good icebreaker for a new group of children to help them get to know each other better.

Gather the children in a circle, and ask the first child to say her name and then name something she would bring on a trip that begins with the first letter of her name. It goes like this: "My name is Nikki. I am going on a trip, and I am bringing nutmeg." The next child does the same thing but adds what the proceeding child said. "My name is Will. I am going on a trip, and I am bringing walnuts. Her name is Nikki, and she's bringing nutmeg." Keep going until every child is introduced. This game is great practice for storing things in short-term memory.

Extension Activities

On our family car rides it was only my sister and I, so it didn't take long to get to know our names. We had to be creative and expand this game to take up more time. Each time it was our turn we had to add another item to bring and remember all the preceding items. It was crazy fun!

Multisensory Explorations

Add some sensory exploration by providing a variety of props to use that would represent the names of all the children in the group (multiple items for each letter would be best). Pick items that are tactile or that make noise to engage more senses.

Diversity Adaptations

Expand the naming to include children's family members to learn different names children have for their parents, grandparents, aunts, uncles, and cousins. They may discover similarities between names and learn ways to relate to each other. You could also pick specific destinations around the world to say where children are going on a trip and ask them to bring something they will need there. "My name is Nikki. I am going to Nicaragua, and I am bringing newspapers."

Would You Rather...?

Intended Ages
four years and older

Brain Connections
expressive and receptive language, critical thinking

Materials Needed
none

When my children were younger, I loved this game. My kids would come up with really good choices. They would ask me things like, "Would you rather have pancakes or french fries for breakfast?" "Would you rather go fishing or to a hockey game?" These were equally nice choices, but the answer depended on my mood. Now that my oldest daughter is a teenager, she plays this game a little differently with me. Now it seems as if her question is always about two bad choices. "Would you rather be poked in the eye or have a horse step on your toe?" (Oh, they grow up so fast.)

When played with young children (ages four and older), this game feels a bit more random. Children will come up with two choices, but there may be no rhyme or reason to them. That's okay. This process begins early, and you keep playing it over time. After they get the hang of it, children begin to develop critical-thinking and deductive reasoning skills. Older children will be able to be more specific about the choices they offer and should be able to ask increasingly complex questions based on the answers. For example, a school-age child might ask, "Would you rather go skiing or swimming?" I say, "Swimming." They say, "Would you rather swim in the ocean or a pool?" I say, "Ocean." They say, "Would you rather swim with dolphins or fish?" See the patterning here? Give it a try.

Extension Activities
Give children who can read and write index cards to write down an object. Have them brainstorm as many objects as possible and make cards for each. Have them generate enough cards for everyone to draw two cards at a time for as many times as you want to play the game. Then invite the children to take turns selecting two random cards, and have them think of a question to ask another member of the group. Say Caitlin draws a pineapple and a turtle. She could ask, "Holly, would you rather dance with a pineapple or a turtle?"

Multisensory Explorations
Gather together a collection of interesting visual aids to help prompt choices between items. Include objects that are varied in texture, smell, size, and shape. Children can sit in a circle and pass a container around with the prompts. Have each child pose a question for another member of the group. "Carlos, would you rather sleep on a rock or a pillow?" Carlos answers, "A rock, of course!" Then it's Carlos's turn to ask the next question.

SOCIAL-EMOTIONAL

Diversity Adaptations

While all this good questioning is going on, look for ways to expand children's worldview. You can ask questions such as, "Would you rather ride a camel or a mule through the desert?" But instead of moving on to another question, begin to elicit open-ended answers. If the answers are off-base (perhaps stereotypical), take this opportunity to redirect the thinking by asking more questions ("Why do you think that?") and providing concrete feedback (correct inaccuracies).

Trust Walk

Intended Ages
five years and older

Brain Connections
perceptual-motor skills

Materials Needed
- blindfolds

Building trust within relationships takes work. I am always amazed that grown-ups often say they don't understand why *this* kid isn't friends with *that* kid. It seems as though even the adult is behaving as if he is three years old. "He likes blue, and she likes blue, so they must be friends!" It's not true for the adult world, and it's not true for the early childhood world. Children need to be able to build trusting relationships with each other just as adults do. Giving children the opportunity to work together—as in taking a trust walk, for example—strengthens the connections within the limbic system, which is the center of emotions.

The children's attention span and how much space you have to walk in will determine just how long your walk will be. Have each child pair up, and have one child be blindfolded. The sighted child will guide the blindfolded child on a walk. For very young children, you really don't need any kind of obstacle course. Being blindfolded is enough of an obstacle as it is. Older children may be able to navigate a simple course of going down a hall, turning a corner, and walking through a doorway. Each child should take turns being blindfolded and leading the other. If possible, encourage the more competent child to be the leader first to model appropriate voice commands (think Zone of Proximal Development).

Extension Activities
This time have all of the children line up with their blindfolds on and hold hands. You (not blindfolded) will be leading the group on a walk while the children are not allowed to talk. See if the children try to help each other in nonverbal ways. Do they instinctively trust the child in front of them to lead them safely on the journey, or do they take timid baby steps? Do they grow more comfortable the longer the walk goes on, or do they become more unsettled? Give it a try!

Multisensory Explorations
This activity is very multisensory already, as the many variations rely on auditory and tactile maneuvering. Perhaps after the children are done with the walk, you could sit them down and have them describe how they felt during the walk. Did they feel safe? Did they feel someone was leading them, or did they feel lost? Older children will be able to reflect more on these questions than younger ones, but ask anyway!

Diversity Adaptations
Individuals from diverse cultural backgrounds may have different views on how trust is

shown. Children will likely adopt their familial mores regarding how trust is demonstrated. Carefully observe children for ways in which they may be demonstrating trust, even if it differs from what you may expect. Typical signs of trust might be one child allowing another to hold a treasured object or inviting another child to play one-on-one. Making eye contact or physical contact could also be signs of trust.

Balance Zone

Intended Ages
four years and older

Brain Connections
perceptual-motor skills

Materials Needed

- comfort items: pillows, blankets, stuffed animals, scarves

- natural objects: bowl of rocks or marbles large enough not to be a choking hazard, tray with sand, leafy plant

- small furniture, if available, in a quiet corner of the room

- books appropriate for the age of the child whose turn it is in the zone

When children spend large portions of their day with other children, they may begin to feel as though they have no boundaries or a place to retreat to when they need some recentering. This activity is designed to offer children the chance to practice creating a balance zone. While nearly all of the activities in this book are designed to work with groups of children at once, this activity is meant to give each child unrushed time without interference to create a place of his own (if only for a short time). You may choose to use your regular comfort area (assuming you have such a place), and that's all right. But what you'll add is materials you might not usually give children unlimited access to. You will be supervising this activity, but you will be doing so from the sideline.

If you have a group of children you are working with, select a time when children are typically engaged in activities on their own (for example, free play). Then choose a child you think might enjoy working in the balance zone. Some children may need encouragement at first, but with each subsequent trip to the zone, they will become more adept at creating their comfort space. Work as closely with the child as you can to get him acclimated to the materials. Very young children will enjoy having the chance to have one-on-one time with you (even if only briefly). Let the other children know you will be available to them in a few minutes, but right now Kevin gets you all to himself.

Ask Kevin questions about where he feels safe. Does he sleep with any stuffed animals at night? Does soft music make him feel good inside? Model to Kevin how you can arrange the pillows and other comfort items to make a space to relax.

When Kevin has lost interest in the zone (or you need to get back to the other children), ask him for permission to dismantle the zone. He may feel that his hard work was destroyed if it is undone by another child. Realizing that most physical space needs to be shared, there is no way to keep a zone in place that is specific for each child. But you can teach a child how to adapt a space to become her zone should she need one. Everyone can use a chance to get away from her workday and her coworkers, even if she is only four years old.

SOCIAL-EMOTIONAL

Extension Activities

Ask parents to bring in a collection of things from home to place in a special box that will be used exclusively for their child. Items could include an article of clothing from a parent that would have her scent on it, a favorite stuffed animal, or a pillow. Depending on the age of the child, he may not want to give up the item to put it back in the box, so use your judgment. Yes, it should remain in the balance zone box, but if the child just isn't ready to let go, give him the time he needs.

Multisensory Explorations

Include materials with distinct scents, such as potpourri (not loose, where a child might eat it, but in a mesh bag). Include satin scarves or tulle, or other fabric with a distinct texture. Use fingertips or a plastic fork to make designs in a tray of sand.

Diversity Adaptations

This activity requires help from families to make each zone unique for each child. Even if parents aren't able to send in materials, ask them to share stories about their home life with you so that you can relate those stories to their child while in the zone. Include pictures of family members and pets for each child and anything else that would make a child feel safe and relaxed.

MUSIC

Brain Connections

Music, it is believed, is cellular. All cultures have music, and many species of animals appear to engage in communication through orchestrated sounds. Few would argue that there isn't music within us. It helps us remember; it gets us moving; it gives us comfort; it entertains; it soothes; it is a gift.

When someone imagines music, it seems her cells are triggered exactly the same way as if she had actually heard music (Sousa 2006). If information can be embedded in music, chances are good it will make its way to long-term memory to be fired up again when the music containing the information is imagined.

Research on music and the effects on the brain can be broken down into two categories: listening to music and producing music. The body and the brain respond in different ways to each of these (Sousa 2006). Listening to music can affect a person's mood, thus creating an emotional response. A person listening to upbeat music may suddenly feel energized or feel her mood improve. Conversely, slow music or tunes with deep resonating beats may cause a person to slow down and be reflective. The benefits can be helpful but short-lived. Passive listening to music does not do as much for the brain as active music creation. The brain must support new motor skills required for the playing of an instrument, as its auditory cortex engages in sound discrimination (Sousa 2006).

Each hemisphere contains areas that respond in distinct ways to both music and language. The left hemisphere, however, contains a special area exclusively for language, and the right hemisphere has a region exclusively for music perception. Getting both sides to work in harmony is important—and also easy. Music is vital to brain-based learning and should be used extensively to enhance learning. But to make what is learned permanent, children must have the opportunity to make their own music.

Music can be used in all of the activities in this book in one way or another. While you are doing a science experiment, you can have background music invigorating your curiosity. Check out Eric Jensen's *Top Tunes for Teaching: 977 Song Titles and Practical Tools for Choosing the Right Music Every Time* (2005) for music suggestions for all occasions.

Supporting Music in the Environment

We want to keep in mind the differences in the way we use music—both to listen to and to create. With that said, it's important to keep a variety of materials on hand for music making as well as listening. As always, I encourage you to add your own to this list, but here are my favorites:

- CD/tape player
- wide variety of recorded music on CD or tape
- cymbals
- drums
- shakers
- bells
- wooden sticks
- harmonica
- accordion
- piano
- guitar
- triangle
- pots, pans, and lids
- wooden spoons
- glass stemware
- paper plates glued together with beans or rice inside
- streamers

Infants and Music

Introducing infants to music is like icing on the cake. For me it's the best part of the cake. Music helps infants develop the ability to discriminate speech patterns and build gross-motor skills, and it provides energizing pickups or soothing calm-downs. It can be used to count music beats, express language, and give directions. Sing songs even if you can't carry a note in a bucket—babies don't care! They will delight in the rhythm and the pattern of your voice. They may enjoy doing the hand movements (even if you are the one holding their hands to make the movements).

Give the babies noisemakers such as rattles, tambourines, bells—things that require only minimal movement to create sound. And when they do, marvel in their achievement! Let them know that you enjoy their music making as much as they do.

Selecting Books for Music

Books about music should have a good variety of rhyming, hold children's attention, and provide extension opportunities to sing the songs after the story is over.

SUGGESTED BOOKS—AGES BIRTH TO FOUR

Greenfield, Eloise. 1992. *I make music*. New York: Writers and Readers Publishing.

Morales, Yuyi. 2008. *Just in case: A trickster tale and Spanish alphabet book*. New York: Roaring Brook Press.

Weatherford, Carole Boston. 2008. *Before John was a jazz giant: A song of John Coltrane*. New York: Henry Holt.

Winter, Jonah. 2006. *Dizzy*. New York: Arthur A. Levine Books.

SUGGESTED BOOKS—AGES FIVE TO EIGHT

Hesse, Karen. 1999. *Come on, rain*. Pictures by Jon J. Muth. New York: Scholastic.

Katz, Alan. 2003. *I'm still here in the bathtub: Brand new silly dilly songs*. Illustrated by David Catrow. New York: Margaret K. McElderry Books.

Nikola-Lisa, W. 1994. *Bein' with you this way*. Illustrated by Michael Bryant. New York: Lee & Low Books.

Winter, Jeanette. 1995. *Follow the drinking gourd*. New York: Alfred A. Knopf.

Head, Shoulders, Knees, and Toes

Intended Ages
two years and older

Brain Connections
receptive and expressive language, perceptual-motor skills

Materials Needed
none

This classic song is great to use as a brain exercise. When the motions are done in a way that has the children cross their hands across their body to touch their body parts, they are able to have cross-lateralization that gets both hemispheres of the brain working together. This song is a great combination of cross-lateralization and perceptual-motor movement (singing and moving). When the song accelerates, children have to improve their coordination and reflexes. Who knew this favorite was such a brain builder?

> Head, shoulders, knees, and toes,
> Knees and toes.
> Head, shoulders, knees, and toes,
> Knees and toes.
> And eyes, and ears, and mouth,
> And nose.
> Head, shoulders, knees, and toes,
> Knees and toes.

Place both hands on the parts of the body as they are sung. Repeat the song and speed up, getting faster with each verse.

While singing the words to the song, use both hands to touch the opposite side of the body part. Left hand touches right shoulder; right hand touches left knee. You get the idea.

Extension Activities
Another great expressive and receptive language song is "Tony Chestnut" by the Learning Station (http://store.learningstationmusic.com/).

Multisensory Explorations
Invite children to pull from dramatic play accessories, or gather up some articles of clothing for children to wear while singing this song. A velour vest would feel soft when the shoulders were touched. Corduroy pants would feel interesting when the knees were touched. How about a clown nose or wig? Get children to use as many of their senses as possible while engaged in physical movement. It helps strengthen those neural connections.

Diversity Adaptations
If you have a foreign language dictionary, a parent who can translate, or access to the Internet, you can generate a list of the names of body parts and make up a new song. Children will be listening for similarities in the sounds of the names in the different languages. Here are some examples.*

ENGLISH	SPANISH	SWAHILI	FRENCH
head	cabeza	kichwa	tête
eyes	ojos	macho	yeux
nose	nariz	pua	nez
mouth	boca	mdomo	bouche
ears	óidos	masikio	oreilles
shoulders	hombres	mabegani	épaules
knees	rodillas	magoti	genoux
toes	dedos de los pies	vidole	orteils

*Google Translate was used to generate this list.

Musical Chairs with a Twist

Intended Ages

five years and older

Brain Connections

receptive and expressive language

Materials Needed

- music
- chairs
- letters, words, or numbers on cards

"Musical chairs" has received a bad rap of late, with talk of emotional harm being done to the child who is left without a seat. I never want to cause harm to a child, and in this activity, there is a chair for each child. This is musical chairs with a twist.

Line up two rows of chairs back to back, one chair for each child. Place a card on each chair with a letter, word, or number on it, depending on what lesson you are supporting. Play music, and have children begin to walk in a circle around the chairs. When the music stops, the children stop in front of a chair, pick up the card on the seat, and read it aloud. The children return the cards to the seats and repeat the game until each child has had a chance to read each note card.

Extension Activities

Place blank cards on the chairs. Children follow the same procedure, but instead of reading the card, they make their own cards. After everyone has a chance to write a word (or letter) on the card, help the children make up a story with the cards.

Multisensory Explorations

Blindfold the children, and have them walk slowly and carefully in a circle with a hand on the shoulder of the person in front of them. Place a variety of objects on the chairs. When the music stops, the children find the object on the chair and identify it from touch.

Diversity Adaptations

Play a variety of world music, including songs sung in other languages. Pick a word out of the song in another language, and have the children stop when they hear that word sung in the song. This will sharpen their auditory discrimination skills.

Rain Sticks

Intended Ages

three years and older

Brain Connections

cause and effect, creative thinking

Materials Needed

- long cardboard tubes about eighteen to twenty-four inches in length, depending on preference (gift wrap paper tubes are excellent, or you can tape several paper towel rolls together)
- marker
- thirty one-inch nails per tube (use nails that have a head, not finishing nails)
- packing or masking tape
- construction paper
- uncooked rice and/or small dried beans

I love the sound of rain coming down on my windowsill. It brings back a flood of memories. But there never seems to be a good rain cloud around when you need one. One solution is to have children make their own rain sticks!

To begin the project, an adult should follow the spiral seam around the paper tube and make about thirty dots a half-inch apart.

Depending on the age of the children, either the child or the adult can gently poke a nail all the way in at each mark, making sure it doesn't poke through the other side. Then use packing or masking tape to wrap around the cardboard tube to hold the nails in place.

Seal off one end of the tube using tape and construction paper. Supply uncooked rice or beans, and allow the child to put a handful of beans or rice or both in the tube. Rice will make a softer sound, while beans will make a harder sound. Securely tape another piece of construction paper over the open end to seal it. When everyone has a stick completed, let the children shake them to hear if they really do sound like rain. The rain stick helps reinforce auditory discrimination skills needed to understand the spoken word as well as sounds associated with letters and objects.

Extension Activities

Try different fillings to see which sounds are more pleasing.

Multisensory Explorations

Use different types of objects, such as metal beads, plastic beads, or buttons, inside the stick to make different sounds. Use any of a variety of materials to cover the outside of the stick—for example, sandpaper, raised glue bumps, pieces of fabric, or natural material such as straw or grass—to create a tactile effect.

Diversity Adaptations

In some places of the world, rain is scarce (Sahara desert), and in other places, it's plentiful (Amazon rain forest) or even hazardous (monsoons in India). Some cultures use rituals during certain seasons to call for rain or to beg for it to stop. After playing with the rain sticks, children can sing, "Rain, rain, go away." And they can put those sticks away for another day.

Hokey Pokey

Intended Ages
two years and older

Brain Connections
perceptual-motor skills, creative thinking

Materials Needed
none

Have you ever wondered if the Hokey Pokey is what it's all about? This classic never gets old. In fact, it can become new and improved by replacing the names of the body parts used.

For example, try the Reindeer Pokey, and put your antlers in and out. Then move up to hooves and bushy tails. It's fun and gets children moving, and you can introduce new vocabulary through the lyrics. Maybe it is what it's all about.

Extension Activities
Have children create antlers to wear while doing the Reindeer Pokey or create other props.

Multisensory Explorations
I was taught how to do the Reindeer Pokey by a Deaf student. She liked this song because she could sign the words in American Sign Language. The words were easy for nonsigners to understand, and it had lots of movement. Combined with our antlers and red noses, this dance used cognitive and motor processing. Now that's what it's all about!

Diversity Adaptations
Use the names of the body parts (partial list provided in the activity Head, Shoulders, Knees, and Toes on page 161) in different languages while you sing the song and do the movements.

Pass the Pattern

Intended Ages

four years and older

Brain Connections

patterning, problem solving, sequencing

Materials Needed

You may be noticing a trend here, but I like activities that require interaction with children. Here is another activity in the same family as "Telephone," but it involves clapping a pattern and passing it along.

Sit with the children in a circle. Start a clapping pattern and demonstrate it to the child next to you. The child repeats your pattern and then demonstrates it to the next child, who passes it on, and so forth. Each person stops after he has handed off the pattern. When the pattern has made its way around the circle, create a new pattern and repeat the process.

Extension Activities

Make the activity more complex by continuing to clap after you have passed on the first clap, and after a few beats, pass around a second pattern. See if the children can continue to pass around two patterns while continuing to clap.

Multisensory Explorations

Use instruments, such as wooden sticks or maracas, to create the pattern. Another variation is to invite children to tap the pattern out on their hands or arms (thighs, hips, belly, backside), instead of clapping or playing an instrument, to further their tactile experience.

Diversity Adaptations

Listen to music from around the world and find songs that use drum beats in tribal dance music or something similar. Do bagpipes have distinct beats? What about a ukulele? Ever watch Riverdance? Pop in a CD, and start jamming to the beat!

MUSIC

Mozart Mania

Intended Ages
four years and older

Brain Connections
patterning, problem solving

Materials Needed

- a CD or cassette of music by Mozart or Bach
- CD or cassette player

You may have heard that having children listen to Mozart will make them smarter. In fact, listening to lots of kinds of music can strengthen neural connections. But some studies have linked improved spatial cognition to listening to Mozart (Sousa 2006). It can't hurt to give it a try. Conduct your own research, and see what kind of effect Mozart has on you. Have the children listen for the four-beats-per-measure rhythm pattern. You may have to help them by counting out loud while clapping to the rhythm yourself. Once they hear the rhythm, encourage them to begin marching and clapping to the beat.

Extension Activities
Try to find as many different genres of music as possible with a four-beat pattern, and have children pick out the similarities.

Multisensory Explorations
Some CD players have a button or control that allows you to boost the bass tones. Find a piece of music (pop or dance music works well) that has a strong four-beat bass rhythm. Boost the bass, and have children put their hands on the CD player to feel the beat.

Diversity Adaptations
While you're marching to the beat of four, count the number of beats in another language. Play music from other cultures with a four-beat rhythm.

Designer Drums

Intended Ages

three years and older

Brain Connections

patterning, perceptual-motor skills

Materials Needed

- oatmeal containers or coffee cans
- plastic wrap
- wax paper
- rubber bands
- rope or cord
- thin rubber sheeting
- balloons
- markers or paint
- fabric
- paper

Do you know some children who seem to march to the beat of a different drummer? Maybe more children would if they could make their own. Give each child an empty container. Depending on the age and skill level of the children, you may need to help individuals in covering the top of the container. Cover the open end of the container with plastic wrap, thick wax paper, fabric, or thin rubber sheeting. Wrap rubber bands around the top of the container to secure the sheeting in place, and make sure it's as tight as possible. Children can then cover the outside of the container with paper and decorate it in any way possible. The rope or cord can be tied around the container to make a lanyard to hold the drum so children's hands are free to drum away!

Extension Activities

After everyone has a drum ready, you can start a marching band. Have the children work together to get a rhythm going, and march to the beat around the room. If the children want to be a rock band instead, have them make guitars out of tissue boxes and empty paper towel rolls. Using an empty rectangular tissue box, wrap rubber bands around the length of the box. Then cut a small hole in one end and insert an empty paper towel roll. Secure the tube with tape or glue. The children can decorate the guitars with paper or paint.

Multisensory Explorations

Once a variety of drums have been created, have children close their eyes and pass the drums around a circle. See if children can identify which drum is theirs by the way it sounds. They will have to use auditory and tactile discrimination, as they rely only on their ears and their hands to pick out their instruments.

Diversity Adaptations

Music is universal and percussion is deeply rooted in many cultures. The process of drum making varies greatly by culture and tradition. Invite guest musicians or drum makers in to talk with children about the history of drum making and how drums are used in different types of music.

MUSIC

The Musical Adventure

Intended Ages
five years and older

Brain Connections
expressive and receptive language, creative thinking

Materials Needed
- variety of instruments, such as maracas, rain sticks, triangles, drums, bells, wind chimes, guitars, sandpaper boards, kazoos, harmonicas, etc.

My daughter Elyse came up with this idea. Children use instruments to provide sound effects for a story. Have children sit in a circle, and let them choose an instrument. Pick a child to start the story (or you can start and model the pattern), and have her use her instrument to create an effect to go along with the tale. For example, "A sailor is on a journey. [beat drum] He sails through a storm." The next child would say, "It started to rain [shakes rain stick]." This goes on until the story is done and everyone has had a chance to make his musical contribution.

Extension Activities
Children can make the sound effects with their mouths to provide effects for the story. For example, "A sailor finds a dolphin [make dolphin noise]."

Multisensory Explorations
Give children a chance to create a book from their story by drawing pictures of their adventure. Each child can draw a picture representing his part of the tale, and all the pages can be assembled into a book.

Diversity Adaptations
This activity combines a lot of diversity adaptations I have already mentioned, like sharing oral histories and discussing instruments from other countries. Continue to do so every chance you get. Having children repeat experiences multiple times helps make connections permanent.

Is the Glass Half Full or Half Empty?

Intended Ages
five years and older

Brain Connections
predicting, cause and effect

Materials Needed
- six glass jars or bottles (per child)
- metal spoon
- wooden spoon
- water

I like to think of myself as a "glass half full" kind of gal—optimistic and upbeat. Speaking of beats, here's a fun way to strengthen auditory discrimination skills. The number of jars or bottles you collect will determine whether each child gets a complete set. I've assumed here each child does.

Give each child a set of glass jars or bottles, and fill each one with a different level of water, leaving one empty. Have the child use a metal spoon to lightly tap on the rim of the bottle to hear the kind of sound it makes. Does the full bottle sound the same as the empty bottle? Does the sound change if you hit the rim with the wooden spoon? Have the children experiment with different water levels and types of spoons to see what kinds of sounds they can create.

Extension Activities
Take this opportunity to have a conversation about pitch (difference between two notes) and notes. What differences can children hear in the pitch between the bottles with different water levels? Children can experiment by adding or reducing water amounts to change the sounds. You can also incorporate math by having children measure the water in ounces or milliliters as they fill the bottles. They can create a chart to record the water amounts that correspond with the notes.

Multisensory Explorations
Does the type of liquid make a difference in sound? What if you changed the liquid to something with a more pungent odor, such as coffee (nothing too hot), lemonade, or tomato juice? Or what if you added something to the liquid, such as marbles, sand, or ice cubes? These changes might create changes in your perception as they affect your senses, but will they actually change the sound? Check it out.

Diversity Adaptations
Use food coloring to change the color of the water in each bottle. Make predictions about what colors will mix together to make another color. How would you know if you were color-blind? In addition to having children create different colors, have them try to describe the different colors in words.

MUSIC

I Can Make It Rain!

Intended Ages

three years and older

Brain Connections

patterning, perceptual-motor skills

Materials Needed

I have the most wonderful memory of being away at summer camp and sitting in the lodge singing songs. Most of the time we sang typical camps songs, such as "John Jacob Jingleheimer Schmidt." But I always looked forward to being able to make it rain inside the lodge. It's not so much a songs, such as as it is a rhythmic pattern of hand rubbing and feet stomping.

With the children sitting, have them start by rubbing the tips of their fingers together to make a soft fluttery sound. After a few seconds, have them move to rubbing their palms together, making an even louder swooshing sound. Then start them briskly clapping their hands on the tops of their thighs, making an even louder patter sound and picking up the pace. Finally, after a few seconds, everyone should quickly stomp his feet loudly, making a thundering sound. And then have the group slowly retreat from the stomping and reverse the order. As they slow down, have the children clap their hands on their thighs and then rub their hands together again even more slowly. Finally, have them rub the tips of their fingers together, slowing down until everyone stops. With a large group, this pattern done in unison sounds like a powerful rainstorm. It's awesome!

Extension Activities

Have children close their eyes and imagine what the rain would feel like if they were out in it. How would it smell? Ask them if they've ever been caught out in the rain before. What did they do? Did the thunder make them scared? Now that they can make rain sounds, will it be less scary the next time they hear it?

Multisensory Explorations

If you can find any, use old-fashioned washboards to make a great thunderstorm noise. Or you could use metal pie tins turned upside. Children can use their hands to drum the tins or a spoon on the washboard to make thundering sounds.

Diversity Adaptations

The rainstorm melody is one that would be heard on a wooden roof. Do all people in the world live under wooden roofs? What would rain sound like on a thatched roof or a metal roof? What about if you lived on the ninth floor of a thirty-four-story building? Would the rain sound the same? Have children brainstorm ways they could change their movements or the objects they rub together to create the illusion of rain hitting different types of roofs.

NATURAL ENVIRONMENT

Brain Connections

Learning how to be protectors of the planet requires skills such as classifying, determining cause and effect, and observing. If we can begin to identify what problems exist in our own environments and possible solutions for how to solve them, we can help the planet *and* help our brains. If we take care of our environment and reduce toxins, we will all have healthier brains. In the *Go Green Rating Scale for Early Childhood Settings* (2010), author Phil Boise uses what he calls the precautionary principle. Boise explains that a young child's brains, organs, and hormones are not yet fully developed and can't properly filter toxins. Therefore, a precautionary principle should be applied when working with young children. "The guiding approach to this *Go Green Rating Scale* program is the precautionary principle, which states that if there is strong evidence that a particular action or material may cause harm, then reduced-risk alternatives to that action or material will be identified and used to the fullest extent possible" (2010, 3). It reminds me of the medical profession's Hippocratic oath, which, when summed up, means "Do no harm."

It's important to remember that our children will inherit this earth. It's imperative that we teach them how to reduce, reuse, and recycle as soon as possible. The activities in this section are designed to help children learn how to be good stewards of the environment. I encourage you to reuse and recycle as many materials as you can for all activities you do with children.

Children do not need the latest, greatest toy from a catalog. They need hands-on experiences using materials they find in their environment, and they need opportunities to see projects develop over time. The life cycles of plants, insects, and animals all help children understand the "big picture" they are a part of. Environmentally friendly activities and long-term projects promote planet awareness and good earth stewardship.

Supporting Natural Environment Studies

You can find lots of ways to support environmental studies by including a variety of materials to further explore both indoors and out. If you have positive memories of time spent in the natural environment, try to share those wonderful memories with children by re-creating those experiences. Here are some of my favorite natural environment elements:

- gardens (sensory and traditional)
- soils (complete with worms)
- recycling containers
- natural cleaning products
- plants
- rocks

I also encourage you to limit your use of disposable products and plastic bags and to reuse materials as many times as possible.

Infants and the Natural Environment

As expert scientists, infants are ready and willing (some more, some less) to explore the natural world around them. While it can be tricky letting very young children explore the natural environment (choking hazards, unsafe surfaces for crawling on, such as wood chips or mulch, sand, etc.), it's still important that babies have a chance to touch, smell, see, hear, and taste their world (they're going to do it anyway!). By being able to touch leaves, babies can feel the textures (veins, stem, dry brittle leaf or firm leaf). They will make connections with those little things hanging on the tree.

By giving infants real objects to explore with, we are helping them make concrete connections with the objects. Watching a caterpillar crawl is an introduction to biology. It is also fun! Go wild.

Selecting Books and Resources for Natural Environment Studies

Choose books that help children develop an appreciation for living creatures and the world around them. Look for books with colorful illustrations and nonstereotypical features of people from around the globe.

SUGGESTED BOOKS—AGES BIRTH TO FOUR

Cronin, Doreen. 2003. *Diary of a worm*. New York: HarperCollins.

———. 2005. *Diary of a spider*. New York: HarperCollins.

Martin, Bill, Jr. 1992. *Brown bear, brown bear, what do you see?* New York: Henry Holt and Company.

Walsh, Melanie. 2008. *10 things I can do to help my world*. Cambridge, MA: Candlewick Press.

SUGGESTED BOOKS—AGES FIVE TO EIGHT

Andreae, Giles, and David Wojtowycz. 1998. *Commotion in the ocean*. New York: Scholastic.

Nussbaum, Hedda. 1979. *Animals build amazing homes*. New York: Random House.

Shulevitz, Uri. 2008. *How I learned geography*. New York: Farrar, Straus and Giroux.

Silverstein, Shel. 1964. *The giving tree*. New York: Harper & Row.

Recycled Art

Intended Ages
three years and older

Brain Connections
creative thinking, sensorimotor skills

Materials Needed
- recycled materials

I remember hearing that everything old is new again (eventually). You can help it come back in vogue sooner with recycled art.

Supply a variety of materials for children to create any kind of art imaginable. Empty paper towel rolls, tissue boxes, wipe containers, and shoe boxes can be used to create instruments. Scraps from magazines, coupon books, and cereal boxes can provide an abundance of text that can be used to create word collages or stories. Children can also create abstract sculptures, murals, or picture collages—you name it. You provide the materials; the masters provide the art!

Extension Activities
Have the projects continue to unfold over time, adding more things as they become available. Create a mural that is added to as more bottle caps are recycled or pictures are taken throughout the year. Or invite children to add their artwork to a class portfolio that is eventually made into a laminated book.

Multisensory Explorations
Be sure to include materials for all the senses. Use scented markers and paint as well as spices. Include as many tactile textures as possible, such as tinfoil, satin, cork, metal, wood, dried flowers, and sand. Include things that are noisy when touched, such as chimes, rustling paper, and squeaky rubber.

Diversity Adaptations
Products that are recycled in the United States may not be the same kinds (or at least in the same quantity) as materials recycled in other countries. When my husband lived in Kenya, he wore sandals made out of recycled tires. He also used discarded metal wire to mold into small toy bicycles. He has fond memories of using a stick to roll a tire and racing against other boys with their wheels. Check out books about the kinds of toys children may use in other countries. One of my favorites is *Elizabeti's Doll* by Stephanie Stuve-Bodeen (1998). Elizabeti has a new baby brother, and she wants a baby of her own to care for. She doesn't have a doll, but she finds a rock that she can cradle and care for. It's heartwarming.

Busy Building Blocks

Intended Ages

one year and older

Brain Connections

sensorimotor skills, creative thinking

Materials Needed

- recycled baby wipe containers

Caring for infants and toddlers leaves me with dozens of plastic baby wipe containers. I felt guilty getting rid of them, even though I wasn't sure what else to do with them. So I did what my mother taught me—stick it in a box and shove it under the table.

One day my best inventors (toddlers) were under the table and discovered the boxes. They began to stack them and play with them like the other large building blocks we had. Hmm . . . problem solved. Children had used their creative thinking skills and helped me problem solve. By adapting these materials into toys, I was able to spare them from reaching the landfill. Children can use these containers for many things, but dumping and filling seem to be a particularly fun use. The bins can be used to sort materials for classifying or playing a sort of memory game. ("I hid a ball in one container. Do you know which one?") The possibilities are endless.

Extension Activities

Collect a variety of recycled containers of different sizes and shapes to expand your recycled block collection.

Multisensory Explorations

Cover recycled baby wipe containers with different textured material to create multisensory building blocks.

Diversity Adaptations

Include diverse fabrics and textures like kente cloth, embroidered silk, and woven tapestry to cover the containers.

Growing Groceries

Intended Ages
two years and older

Brain Connections
predicting, observing, receptive and expressive language

Materials Needed
- pots for growing plants
- potting soil
- seeds for plants

Long-term projects require prolonged contact with materials (which strengthens connections), divergent thinking skills (which builds creative and flexible thinking), and delayed gratification (which is controlled by executive function and involves self-regulation). Try growing plants that can be used to create a specific meal. Grow tomatoes, basil, and onions to make homemade pasta sauce. Or how about planting pumpkin seeds and making your own pie? For more ideas like this, check out the book *Early Sprouts* (Kalich, Bauer, and McPartlin 2009).

Do some research to find out what kind of groceries you want to grow. Will the ingredients for marinara sauce grow well in your garden? Do you get the right kind of light, rainfall, and temperature to produce the kind of plants you want to grow? If so, plant away. It will take a growing cycle to net the groceries, so be prepared to wait.

Help children understand how the plant growth cycle works. Emphasize the value of buying groceries from local markets to reduce the impact of carbon emissions from trucks carrying our food from great distances.

Extension Activities
During the growing period, talk about the types of plants you are growing. Talk about any problems that might come up. Have the children help tend the garden daily or weekly. Keep written schedules for watering and fertilizing, if necessary. Have a target date for a harvest party.

Multisensory Explorations
Choose very fragrant plants to enjoy during the growing cycle. Allow children to feel the leaves or stems of the food as it grows.

Diversity Adaptations
Invite parents to participate in the celebratory meal. Have children create decorations surrounding the meal theme. If you made spaghetti sauce, celebrate Italy. If you made salsa, celebrate Mexico.

Mary, Mary, Quite Contrary, How Does Your Garden Grow?

Intended Ages
three years and older

Brain Connections
sensorimotor skills, predicting, cause and effect, creative thinking

Materials Needed
- four- or six-inch clay saucer
- potting soil
- grass seeds
- spray bottle
- twigs
- rocks
- shells
- dry flowers

Watching the grass grow has never been so much fun! In many early childhood settings, even a small patch is hard to come by. Here's a chance to create a green patch of your very own and turn it into a special desktop garden.

Visit a local nursery and get some small clay saucers (the kind pots sit in). Fill the saucers with potting soil, sprinkle with quick-growing grass seed, and sit back and watch the grass grow. Add some twigs, dried flowers, small rocks, or an upside-down shell to hold water like a pond, and create a dish garden you can enjoy indoors.

Watching the little gardens grow will strengthen observation skills and a better understanding of cause and effect. The gardens will need continual care, as the grass will need to be watered (and perhaps trimmed with little scissors).

This little garden dish makes an excellent metaphor for brain development. When cared for and given a stimulating environment, the brain can thrive. Eventually some dendrites sprout but don't make a connection and need to be pruned.

Extension Activities
Plant a larger patch of grass in a larger container or flat tray. Infants and toddlers are often uncomfortable the first time they are plopped down in the yard, so a little patch of grass on the ground inside could help them get used to the touch. Choose a tray big enough for a toddler to sit in.

Multisensory Explorations
Select a pungent grass, such as lemongrass, or plant other "smelly" plants in your garden, such as catnip, cilantro, lavender, tarragon, and mint.

Diversity Adaptations
If you can, grow different kinds of grass that could be found in different climates. Add flowers from different countries to create pots that reflect different cultures.

Bird food feeders

Intended Ages
three years and older

Brain Connections
creative thinking

Materials Needed
- homemade paste (one cup flour, one cup water)
- birdseed
- wax paper
- string for hanging

I used to cringe every time one of my children would come home with a bird feeder slathered in peanut butter. Since when did peanut butter become a staple of an oriole's diet? I had to put a stop to that right away. I couldn't stand to think of those little orange birds having peanut butter stuck to the roof of their beaks.

Instead, have children use flour and water to make a homemade flour paste. Help children mix the flour and water; add more water or flour until the paste is smooth. Demonstrate for children how to use the homemade flour paste to create a pretzel shape on wax paper, and then sprinkle it with birdseed. Allow the flour paste to dry for a day or two; then peel off the paper and hang the pretzel outside for your feathered friends. Make predictions about how long it will take before the birds find the feeders. Document observations that are made about how the birds respond to the feeders.

Extension Activities
Use different types of birdseed to draw a variety of birds to the area. Keep a chart to record the types of birds observed.

Multisensory Explorations
Do some research to find out if birds in your area are attracted to certain kinds of trees, plants, or flowers, and add branches or leaves from those plants to the feeder.

Diversity Adaptations
Obviously you will only attract those birds that hang around your area, but you can study what types of birds live in other parts of the world and what they might eat as a part of their diet.

Green Map

Intended Ages
six years and older

Brain Connections
classifying, comparing

Materials Needed
- large sheet of paper
- pencils
- ruler
- crayons (blue, green, brown, or more)

Everyone's talking about going green, but is it working? If you have been recycling, reusing, and reducing, has it had an impact yet? What are your neighbors doing to save the planet? Make a green map to find out.

Make a map of your neighborhood (or town or county, depending on how large or small you want your map to be), highlighting the eco-friendly areas and the toxic areas. Indicate places that support wildlife, recycling, and gardens on the map. Once you have a visual indicator of how effective the green movement has been in your area, have children brainstorm ideas of ways to increase the green zones. Can they chip in to start a neighborhood recycling program? What about planting trees or planting a garden? Once children become invested in a project, their limbic system will get involved and strengthen their emotional connection.

Extension Activities
Make a map of your state or region, and highlight similar areas. Visit www.greenmap.com to get ideas about making green maps.

Multisensory Explorations
Make topographical maps with textured surfaces representing each earth-friendly area.

Diversity Adaptations
What does being green mean in other countries? Make a green map of the planet.

Recycled Scoops

Intended Ages
four years and older

Brain Connections
problem solving, creative thinking

Materials Needed
- recycled plastic gallon jugs (or smaller)
- duct tape
- hot glue (if necessary)
- box cutter or sharp knife
- wax paper
- permanent markers
- yarn, Velcro or other textured material for handle grip

Start with a clean, recycled bottle with the cap intact (you can hot-glue some caps if you don't want them to accidentally come off). Use a box cutter or sharp knife to cut the gallon jugs. Use a permanent marker to draw your cut lines first. You will want to leave the handle on the bottle to make it the scoop handle. If you want to leave the cap on the bottle to use it as a funnel, cut a hole in the bottom of the bottle. If you want a solid bottom to the scoop, then cut off the top where the cap is leaving the handle intact. Do not let children attempt to cut the container!

Use duct tape to cover the cut edges of the bottle, or use heat to slightly melt the edge and rub with wax paper to create a smooth edge. Allow children to label or decorate the scoops however they like. Once scoops are completed, children will be able to use them as tools. This sounds simple enough and not very extraordinary, but it is. Children will be able to be better problem solvers if they know how to use a variety of tools. Tools are meant to make complex or difficult work easier. When children learn to determine when they need help, where to go find it, and how to select the proper tools, they are developing valuable critical-thinking skills. When children use these scoops decorated with tactile features, it will stimulate their senses and help strengthen the connection to whatever the child needed the tool for. The use of tools can become an extension of their neural network.

Extension Activities
Make scoops of different sizes for different sizes of hands and different types of tasks. Smaller children will want to use these scoops but might not be able to carry a big scoop full of something (such as sand or beans).

Multisensory Explorations
Decorate the outside of the container to create different surfaces for different uses of the scoops. Add a grip to the handle so it doesn't slip out of little hands during water play.

Diversity Adaptations
You can use different types of materials to create bowls or scoops to resemble containers found in different countries. You can experiment and make bowls or scoops out of dried gourds or clay. You can also use straps or other handles to attach to the plastic jug scoops to make them easier to use for those with differing abilities.

Recycled Wrapping Paper

Intended Ages

three years and older

Brain Connections

sensorimotor skills, creative thinking

Materials Needed

- various kinds of recycled paper
- print makers (potato mashers, cookie cutters, etc.)
- tempera paint
- smocks to protect clothing
- wrapping paper tubes

This activity reminds me of a scene from an old movie called *Splash* (1984). Tom Hanks gives Darryl Hannah (a mermaid) a gift. She's never seen a gift before, so she doesn't know that the wrapped package is supposed to be opened. When he hands her the nicely wrapped gift, she begins to gush that this is the most beautiful thing anyone has ever given her before. He then has to explain that she has to open the box, and she can't believe there is something more than this nicely wrapped gift. When children make their own gift wrap, their parents won't want to open the gifts either.

Gather recycled paper materials, such as tissue paper, newsprint, or paper bags. Spread out the paper, and use everyday kitchen items, such as a potato masher, cookie cutters, or dessert molds, to create prints using tempera paint. Help children think of ways they want to use their paper before they begin creating, so they can make a plan for what they are going to do. This gets them thinking creatively but also thinking critically about the purpose of the design and how the paper will be used. Leave the paper out to dry, and if possible roll the paper on recycled wrapping paper tubes for later use.

Extension Activities

Use other recycled materials for bows, ribbons, and tags.

Multisensory Explorations

Include embellishments (buttons, sequins, glitter, sparkles, etc.) that have raised surfaces for decorating the paper and the bows, ribbons, and tags.

Diversity Adaptations

Include paper and graphic designs from different cultures (many examples have been provided in the art section under diversity adaptations). You can also use recycled cloth or plastic to create a different kind of wrapping "paper."

NATURAL ENVIRONMENT

Homemade Butter

Intended Ages

two years and older

Brain Connections

sensorimotor skills, memory, cause and effect

Materials Needed

- heavy whipping cream (room temperature works best)
- salt (optional)
- pint jar with a secure lid
- crackers or bread

Helping children understand the genesis of items they use will embed the understanding of these items in their memory. Making butter, applesauce, and playdough cements the connections about these items in our brains. And butter is yummy, so let's make some.

Add heavy cream and a pinch of salt (optional) to a pint jar. Have the children each take a turn to vigorously shake, roll, jiggle, or do whatever motion works best until cream is stiff. This could take as long as fifteen minutes, depending on the rigor of the jiggle. Once the butter is ready, it should be enjoyed! Offer children the chance to taste the butter on crackers or bread. Having children connect the memory of this activity with a sense like taste will help it stick.

Extension Activities

Make other items, such as ice cream, in a bag (recipe follows), which requires much of the same movement, so children can build on prior learning. Keep in mind that if you have any children with food allergies (specifically lactose) avoid using dairy products by using soy based products.

one-gallon and one-quart resealable bag (heavy duty)

four cups ice

one-quarter cup kosher salt

one cup whole milk

one teaspoon vanilla (or other flavoring)

two tablespoons sugar

cups and spoons

Add the whole milk, flavoring, and sugar to the quart-size bag. Seal it up tightly, making sure to get out as much air as possible. In the gallon bag put the salt, ice, and the quart-size bag. Each child will need to briskly shake the bags together to allow the ice cream to form. You could also put the sealed plastic bags in a container or coffee can to make it easier to shake vigorously. It will take approximately ten minutes of shaking for the ice cream to form.

Multisensory Explorations

Add scents or different flavors (cookie crumbles, chocolate pieces) to the butter or ice cream to add taste and smell experiences.

Diversity Adaptations

Use different kinds of milk (such as goat's milk or soy milk) to relate to different tastes and cultures.

Water Works

Intended Ages
five years and older

Brain Connections
problem solving, critical thinking

Materials Needed
- poster board or flip chart paper
- markers
- ruler

Everyone needs water, and for some people it can be more scarce or more expensive than you'd think. We needed to help educate our children about water conservation.

To help children be able to see how much water they are using for different purposes, make a chart to record measurements of the water you use. Use a large piece of poster board or flip chart paper and use a ruler to make a graph. Include the categories you are tracking on the left side and then make a row to record the dates across the top. In each box for the activity and date, you will record the amount of usage. You can either do this for each child individually or as a group.

In order to calculate usage, record the amount of time the water is running and then determine what your use is per minute. Your local water utility can tell you this if you don't know. You can also use www.waterfootprint.org to help you calculate your use. After a week of recording consumption, children can discuss what they thought about their usage and, if necessary, brainstorm ways to cut back. For the next week, implement the conservation techniques and record the new measurements. At the end of the second week, compare the records and see if there has been a reduction in use.

Extension Activities
Have the children create a diagram showing the water cycle in your area. Do you have mountain runoff? Live near an ocean? How far does your water have to travel to reach your tap? What kinds of things does it go through before it gets to your kitchen? Each child can draw a different part of the cycle, and you can create a mural of how the whole system works together.

Multisensory Explorations
Playing in water is a wonderful multisensory experience. Keep that water table (or other container) where children can practice dumping and filling buckets of water, measuring, and pouring, put try ways to conserve the water you use. Use the least amount you can to practice skills. Teach children how to respect the water by not dumping it out on the ground, and cover the water table when you're finished so it doesn't evaporate too quickly. But by all means, enjoy the wonderful wetness of water!

Diversity Adaptations
Unfortunately, there are currently more people on the planet who have contaminated drinking water than people who have safe drinking water. Teach children to value natural

resources like clean drinking water, and help them learn ways to help others. Living Water International is one organization that helps villages across the globe install pumps and filtration systems to purify their water. You can learn more about Living Water International by visiting www.water.cc.

UNICEF has been instrumental in helping communities develop ways to carry clean drinking water and develop sustainable systems for maintaining safe water. To learn more about UNICEF, visit www.unicef.org.

One activity you could try to help children understand what life might be like in other countries could be to help them establish a rainwater collection system. Have children talk about what their water needs are in their classroom community. Water in this case won't be used for drinking water. However, if you've decided to grow gardens and flowers, you would be able to help children experience what it might be like to have to carry the water from the collection site to the area where water is needed. Collect large plastic containers that can be placed under rain gutter downspouts to collect rainwater. After a rain, children can take turns (using buckets the children have made or collected) carrying the water to the garden or plants or water table. Read stories about ways rain is collected and about local water systems in different geographic locations. Invite guests with knowledge of water usage and needs to come and talk to children and help them brainstorm ways children can become involved in water sustainability projects.

ACTIVITY	LANGUAGE	MATHEMATICS	SCIENCE	ART	MOTOR SKILLS	SOCIAL-EMOTIONAL DEVELOPMENT	MUSIC	NATURAL ENVIRONMENT
LANGUAGE								
My Favorite Story!				■		■		
What Came First?		■		■				
Alpha Box		■	■			■		
Magic Writing				■	■			
Sensory Scribbles					■	■		
Bag o' Wonder			■		■	■		
Rhyming Scavenger Hunt					■			
Flannel Fantasy					■	■		
Fingerplays						■	■	
Deciphering Decibels			■					
MATHEMATICS								
Pitter-Pat Patterns	■				■		■	
Ten in the Bed Counting Sticks	■				■			
Patchwork Patterns	■				■	■		
One of These Things Is Not Like the Other	■				■			
Budding Builders	■		■		■			
Everyday Math	■					■		
Big Shoes to Fill			■	■				
Fraction Food					■	■		
Subatize!	■					■		
Petals around the Rose	■							

ACTIVITY

	LANGUAGE	MATHEMATICS	SCIENCE	ART	MOTOR SKILLS	SOCIAL-EMOTIONAL DEVELOPMENT	MUSIC	NATURAL ENVIRONMENT
SCIENCE								
Tubular Flatulence	■			■				
What Happens If…?	■			■		■		
Sensory Exchange	■			■	■	■	■	
Bottled Up from the Bottom Up	■			■				■
Delicious DNA		■		■	■			
Evaporation Exploration				■				
You Are What You Eat								■
Rotation and Relation	■	■		■				
Sensory Squares	■			■				
Secret Scents	■			■				
Flash Cards				■				
ART								
Homemade Scratch-and-Sniff Books			■	■		■		■
What's in the Bag?			■			■		■
Doable Dough		■	■					
Upside-Down Art			■		■			
Sand Painting with Salt			■					
Pasta Pictures	■	■						
Stained-Glass Pictures		■						■
Bubble Paintings			■		■	■		
Drawing in the Dark						■	■	

ACTIVITY	LANGUAGE	MATHEMATICS	SCIENCE	ART	MOTOR SKILLS	SOCIAL-EMOTIONAL DEVELOPMENT	MUSIC	NATURAL ENVIRONMENT
MOTOR SKILLS								
Follow the Language Leader	■	■						
Obstacle Course, of Course		■						
Pass the Pretzel, Please		■				■	■	
R Is for Reverse	■							
Balance Beam			■				■	
Walking the Walk and Talking the Talk	■					■		
Animals on the Move		■	■	■				
What's Cookin'?				■		■		
Who Am I?	■					■		
Back-to-Back Ball	■					■		
SOCIAL AND EMOTIONAL DEVELOPMENT								
Silhouette Self-Portrait	■			■				
Pass the Face				■	■			
What's All the Hoopla?						■	■	
Mood Mask				■				■
Puppets as People				■				
Tude O'Meter				■				
Going on a Trip	■				■			
Would You Rather…?	■							
Trust Walk					■			
Balance Zone								■

ACTIVITY	LANGUAGE	MATHEMATICS	SCIENCE	ART	MOTOR SKILLS	SOCIAL-EMOTIONAL DEVELOPMENT	MUSIC	NATURAL ENVIRONMENT
MUSIC								
Head, Shoulders, Knees, and Toes					■	■		
Musical Chairs with a Twist	■				■			
Rain Sticks			■	■				■
Hokey Pokey					■			
Pass the Pattern					■			
Mozart Mania		■			■			
Designer Drums				■	■			
The Musical Adventure	■				■			
Is the Glass Half Full of Half Empty?		■	■					
I Can Make it Rain!					■			
NATURAL ENVIRONMENT								
Recycled Art				■				
Busy Building Blocks				■				
Growing Groceries	■	■	■		■			
Mary, Mary Quite Contrary, How Does Your Garden Grow?			■	■	■	■		
SOCIAL/EMOTIONAL DEVELOPMENT								
Bird Food Feeders		■	■	■				
Green Map	■	■	■	■				
Recycled Scoops				■				
Recycled Wrapping Paper				■				
Homemade Butter		■	■					
Water Works			■					

GLOSSARY

assessment

a process to determine the progress of a student to find out how effective instruction has been

attunement

giving attention to a subject for a period of time

automaticity

attention that is nonconscious

axons

long fibers extending from brain cells (neurons) that carry output information in the form of an electric impulse

brain-based learning

a learning theory based on current neuroscience that focuses on the structure and function of the brain as it relates to learning

cerebral cortex

outermost layer of the cerebrum; it is wrinkled, looks like a rind, has six layers, and is packed with brain cells.

cerebral hemispheres (left and right)

the two main sections of the brain responsible for different functions. The left hemisphere is primarily responsible for language processing and higher-order thinking (like the ability to retrieve facts and organize thoughts). The right hemisphere works more randomly and processes using whole systems (integrating perceptual input).

concrete words

words that have real meaning to young children. Usually these are the first words a child can "read" (recognizing the words' letters and sounds) because of the meaning these words hold for the child; examples include a child's own name and the names of Mommy, Daddy, a sibling, and a pet or favorite toy.

corpus callosum

a broad, thick band in the brain connecting the hemispheres and consisting of millions and millions of nerve fibers, which are axons of cells in the cerebral cortex

dendrites

highly complex, branching structures in the brain that form the major receiving part of neurons, within which the real work of the nervous system takes place, where thousands of synaptic inputs from other neurons are received in reading and comprehension of written and oral language

emotional intelligence

a theory by Daniel Goleman, derived from Howard Gardner's theory of multiple intelligences, that considers how much the influence of feelings contributes to our learning

enriched environment

a setting with opportunities for learning that maximize brain-based learning

frontal lobe

the front portion of the cerebral hemisphere in the brain whose motor areas control movements of the voluntary skeletal muscles and whose association areas carry on higher intellectual processes, such as concentration, planning, problem solving, and judging the consequences of behavior

limbic system

a complex set of structures midbrain (above and around the thalamus and just under the cerebrum) that includes the hypothalamus, the hippocampus, the amygdala, and several other nearby areas and appears to be responsible primarily for our emotional life and to have much to do with formatting memories

logographic

a simple symbol or picture that acts as a visual reminder of an important literary element in a text, thereby providing a support for students as they read

memory

where information such as recollections, facts, and images, are stored. There are different locations in the brain for memory for different types of data stored.

automatic/reflexive memory
holds things you know automatically because of high frequency use, such as names, sounds, and letters

emotional memory

stores positive and negative feelings and can recall the feelings when triggered by an emotional event

episodic memory

accessed when one stimulus generates a mental response related to the stimulus (for example, a few words of a song make you remember where you were the first time you heard it). Episodic memory is triggered by a prompt from automatic memory.

long-term memory

occurs in the frontal lobes, where it is determined what information is retained; that information is sorted and sent to learning and memory. It includes explicit memories, which are intentional, conscious recollections of experience.

procedural memory

where information is consistently repeated until it becomes automatic

short-term memory

memory that can hold seven pieces of information (plus or minus two) at a time

working memory

memory that holds some number of units of information for only five to twenty seconds

myelination

the process that occurs in the brain when the axons are coated with myelin, which allows the nerve impulses to travel faster

neurons

one of two types of brain cells that receive stimulation from the dendrites. Over 100 billion neurons are in the human brain.

occipital lobe

forming the back portion of each cerebral hemisphere and separated from the cerebellum by a shelflike extension, called the tentorium cerebelli. There is no distinct boundary between the occipital lobe and the parietal lobe in front of it, nor with the temporal lobe that lies under it. The occipital lobe's sensory areas are responsible for vision; the associated regions function to combine visual images with other sensory experiences.

parietal lobe

located just behind the frontal lobe in each cerebral hemisphere and separated from the hemispheres by a shallow groove with sensory regions responsible for the sensations of temperature, touch, pressure, and pain from the skin and association areas functioning in understanding speech and in using words to express thoughts and feelings

pragmatics

the use of language in social contexts, such as knowing what to say, how to say it, and when to say it

pruning

the process by which the brain sheds unformed neurological connections to make way for concrete thinking during several phases in a person's life span

scaffolding

providing support to learners as they stack or build on existing knowledge as new experiences are gained

schema

our reference for meaning based on prior experience

self-regulation (will and skill)

students' ability to understand and control their learning and match their will for learning to their skill for learning

semantic

pertaining to the meaning of words

semantics

the study of the meanings of words

synapse

a small gap separating a neuron's dendrites and axons, across which impulses flow from one neuron to another

temporal lobe

located in the brain below the frontal lobe of the cerebral hemisphere and separated from it by a shallow groove. Sensory areas located here are responsible for hearing and association areas used in the interpretation of sensory experiences and in the memory of visual scenes, music, and other complex sensory patterns.

visual perception

information that is processed visually

Zone of Proximal Development (ZPD)

Lev Vygotsky's theory that describes the range of tasks a child can do with the help of an adult or skilled peer

REFERENCES

Amen, Daniel G. 1998. *Change your brain, change your life: The breakthrough program for conquering anxiety, depression, obsessiveness, anger, and impulsiveness.* New York: Times Books.

Balkwill, Frances R., and Mic Rolph. 1993. *Cells are us.* Minneapolis: Carolrhoda Books.

———. 1994. *Amazing schemes within your genes.* Minneapolis: Carolrhoda Books.

———. 1994. *DNA is here to stay.* Minneapolis: Carolrhoda Books.

———. 2001. *Enjoy your cells.* Cold Spring Harbor, NY: Cold Spring Harbor Laboratory Press.

———. 2002. *Have a nice DNA.* Cold Spring Harbor, NY: Cold Spring Harbor Laboratory Press.

Bardige, Betty S., and Marilyn M. Segal. 2005. *Poems to learn to read by: Building literacy with love.* Washington, DC: Zero to Three Press.

Blakemore, Sarah-Jayne, and Uta Frith. 2005. *The learning brain: Lessons for education.* Malden, MA: Blackwell Publishing.

Bodrova, Elena, and Deborah J. Leong. 2007. *Tools of the mind: The Vygotskian approach to early childhood education.* 2nd ed. Upper Saddle River, NJ: Pearson/Merrill Prentice Hall.

Boise, Phil. 2010. *Go green rating scale for early childhood settings.* St. Paul: Redleaf Press.

Bronfenbrenner, Urie. 1981. *The ecology of human development: Experiments by nature and design.* Cambridge, MA: Harvard University Press.

Caine, Renate Nummela, and Geoffrey Caine. 1994. *Making connections: Teaching and the human brain.* Menlo Park, CA: Addison-Wesley.

Caine, Renate Nummela, Geoffrey Caine, Carol McClintic, and Karl J. Klimek. 2009. *12 brain/mind learning principles in action: Developing executive functions of the human brain.* 2nd ed. Thousand Oaks, CA: Corwin Press.

Center on the Social and Emotional Foundations for Early Learning Web site. 2009. Vanderbilt University. http://www.vanderbilt.edu/csefel.

Coles, Robert, ed. 2000. *The Erik Erikson reader*. New York: W. W. Norton.

Connell, J. Diane. 2005. *Brain-based strategies to reach every learner*. New York: Scholastic.

Cox, Adam J. 2007. *No mind left behind: Understanding and fostering executive control—the eight essential brain skills every child needs to thrive*. New York: Penguin.

Cunningham, Patricia M. 2004. *Phonics they use: Words for reading and writing*. 4th ed. Boston: Pearson/Allyn & Bacon.

Daniels, H. 1994. *Literature Circles: Voice and choice in the student-centered classroom*. Markham, ON, Canada. Pembroke Publishers Ltd.

Dennison, Paul E., and Gail E. Dennison. 1986. *Brain gym: Simple activities for whole brain learning*. Glendale, CA: Edu-Kinesthetics.

Derman-Sparks, Louise, and the ABC Task Force. 1989. *Anti-bias curriculum: Tools for empowering young children*. Washington, DC: National Association for the Education of Young Children.

Eliot, Lise. 2000. *What's going on in there? How the brain and mind develop in the first five years of life*. New York: Bantam Books.

Feldman, Jean. 2009. Web site: http://www.drjean.org.

Fox, Mem. 2001. *Reading magic: Why reading aloud to our children will change their lives forever*. Illustrations by Judy Horacek. New York: Harcourt.

Gardner, Howard. 2004. *Frames of Mind*. New York: Basic Books.

Goleman, Daniel. 1995. *Emotional intelligence*. New York: Bantam.

Goodwyn, S. W., L. P. Acredolo, and C. Brown. 2000. "Impact of symbolic gesturing on early language development." *Journal of Nonverbal Behavior* 24:81–103.

Gopnik, Alison, Andrew N. Meltzoff, and Patricia K. Meltzoff. 1999. *The scientist in the crib: Minds, brains, and how children learn*. New York: William Morrow.

Guhin, Paula. 2001. *Can we eat the art? Incredible edibles and art you can't eat*. Nashville: Incentive Publications, Inc.

Hansen, Harlan, and Ruth Hansen. 2009. *Lessons for literacy: Promoting preschool success*. St. Paul: Redleaf Press.

Helm, Judy H., and Lilian Katz. 2001. *Young investigators: The project approach in the early years*. New York: Teachers College Press.

Hill, Linda D. 2001. *Connecting Kids: Exploring Diversity Together*. Gabriola Island, BC, Canada: New Society Publishers.

Jalongo, Mary Renck. 2004. *Young children and picture books*. 2nd ed. Washington, DC: National Association for the Education of Young Children.

Jensen, Eric. 1998. *Teaching with the brain in mind*. Alexandria, VA: Association for Supervision and Curriculum Development.

———. 2004. *Brain-compatible strategies: Hundreds of easy-to-use, brain-compatible activities that boost attention, motivation, learning and achievement.* 2nd ed. San Diego: Brain Store.

———. 2005. *Top tunes for teaching: 977 song titles and practical tools for choosing the right music every time.* San Diego: Brain Store.

———. 2007. *Introduction to brain-compatible learning.* 2nd ed. Thousand Oaks, CA: Corwin Press.

———. 2008. *Brain-based learning: The new paradigm of teaching.* 2nd ed. Thousand Oaks, CA: Corwin Press.

Johnson, Jeff A., and Tasha A. Johnson. 2006. *Do-it-yourself early learning: Easy and fun activities and toys from everyday home center materials.* St. Paul: Redleaf Press.

Johnson, Jeff A., with Zoë Johnson. 2008. *Everyday early learning: Easy and fun activities and toys from stuff you can find around the house.* St. Paul: Redleaf Press.

Jones, Elizabeth, and Renatta M. Cooper. 2006. *Playing to get smart.* Early childhood education series. New York: Teachers College Press.

Jones, Elizabeth, and Gretchen Reynolds. 1992. *The play's the thing: Teachers' roles in children's play.* Early childhood education series. New York: Teachers College Press.

Kalich, Karrie, Dottie Bauer, and Deirdre McPartlin. 2009. *Early sprouts: Cultivating healthy food choices in young children.* St. Paul: Redleaf Press.

Karges-Bone, Linda. 1998. *More than pink and blue: How gender can shape your curriculum.* Illustrated by Darcy Tom. Carthage, IL: Teaching & Learning.

Katz, Lawrence C., and Manning Rubin. 1999. *Keep your brain alive: 83 neurobic exercises to help prevent memory loss and increase mental fitness.* New York: Workman.

Kostelink, Marjorie J., Anne K. Soderman, and Alice P. Whiren. 2007. *Developmentally appropriate curriculum: Best practices in early childhood education.* 4th ed. Upper Saddle River, NJ: Pearson/Merrill Prentice Hall.

Maslow, Abraham H. 1966. *The psychology of science: A reconnaissance.* New York: Harper & Row.

Medina, John J. 2008. *Brain rules: 12 principles for surviving and thriving at work, home, and school.* Seattle: Pear Press.

Miller, George A. 1956. "The magical number seven, plus or minus two: some limits on our capacity for processing information." *Psychological Review* 63, no. 2: 81–97. http://psychclassics.yorku.ca/Miller/.

Offutt, Elizabeth Rhodes. 1997. *An elementary teacher's guide to multiple intelligences.* Torrance, CA: Good Apple.

Owocki, Gretchen. 1999. *Literacy through play.* Portsmouth, NH: Heinemann.

Paley, Vivian Gussin. 2004. *A child's work: The importance of fantasy play.* Chicago: University of Chicago Press.

Reynolds, Gretchen, and Elizabeth Jones. 1997. *Master players: Learning from children at play.* Early childhood education series. New York: Teachers College Press.

Schiller, Pam. 1999. *Start smart! Building brain power in the early years.* Beltsville, MD: Gryphon House.

Schilling, Dianne. 1996. *50 activities for teaching emotional intelligence: Level 1, grades 1–5 elementary school.* Carson, CA: Innerchoice Publishing.

Seuss, Dr. 1990. *Oh, The Places You'll Go!* New York: Random House.

Sousa, David A. 2003. *How the gifted brain learns.* Thousand Oaks, CA: Corwin Press.

———. 2005. *How the brain learns to read.* Thousand Oaks, CA: Corwin Press.

———. 2006. *How the brain learns.* 3rd ed. Thousand Oaks, CA: Corwin Press.

———. 2007. *How the special needs brain learns.* 2nd ed. Thousand Oaks, CA: Corwin Press.

Strickland, Susan J. 2001. *Childhood Education,* 78 no. 2: 100(4) Association for Childhood Education International.

Stuve-Bodeen, Stephanie. 1998. *Elizabeti's doll.* Illustrated by Christy Hale. New York: Lee and Low Books.

Tramo, Mark Jude. 2001. "Biology and music enhanced: Music of the hemispheres." *Science* 291, no. 5501: 54–56.

Tileston, Donna Walker. 2005. *10 best teaching practices: How brain research, learning styles, and standards define teaching competencies.* 2nd ed. Thousand Oaks, CA: Corwin Press.

Whelan, Mary Steiner. 2000. *But they spit, scratch, and swear! The do's and don'ts of behavior guidance with school-age children.* Minneapolis: A-ha! Communications.

Wurm, Julianne P. 2005. *Working in the Reggio way: A beginner's guide for American teachers.* St. Paul: Redleaf Press.

ABOUT THE AUTHOR

Nikki Darling-Kuria was the first nationally accredited family child care provider in the state of Maryland by the National Association for Family Child Care in 2001. She won the *Early Childhood Today* Early Childhood Educator of the Year Award in 2005.

Nikki serves as the communications chair for NAFCC, teaches activities for young children and school-age children at a community college in Maryland, and is currently a registered and accredited family child care provider in West Virginia. She will complete her master's degree in human development in the spring of 2010.

Nikki lives with her husband of nineteen years who is a native of Kenya, her three beautiful children, an old beagle, a young black Labrador retriever, and a variety of dust bunnies that she is too busy to chase away.